"Stripped is a bare-kn_____ _____y business."
— *Scott Dickensheets, Las Vegas Weekly*

"The body parts litter the stage as Jordan gives Galardi's gang the samurai sword treatment...I suspect it also will be required reading for defense attorneys and prosecutors alike in the ugly Galardi affair."
— *John L. Smith, Las Vegas Review Journal*

"...a scathing book based on his 12 years as a bouncer and doorman at Cheetahs...he's the only person associated with the business willing to talk publicly..."
— *George Knapp, Ch. 8 Las Vegas*

"He named names in his tell-all book, and a lot of people are angry."
— *Jessica Del Curto, Daily Lobo*

"...violating civil rights, facilitating political corruption, acting as a strong-arm robber, delivering violent beatings and falsifying police reports were part of his job description..."
— *Jhen Kordela, Daily Aztec*

"Brent Jordan, [was] a long-time bouncer at Cheetah's Las Vegas, who was there to see it all as the FBI gathered evidence for Operation G-Sting."
— *Darcy Spears, KVBC, News 3 Las Vegas*

"A breezy yet disturbing work...Jordan succeeds wildly, blending the occasionally grizzly aspects of his often rough-and-tumble job with a marvelously fluid and chatty writing style."
— *Mac VerStandig, The Badger Herald*

"There are many passages in the book that will offend some and a few that may even make you shake your head in disbelief and say I can't believe they do that. For those who have never been to a strip club, it is an eye-opening and interesting perspective that Jordan places you."
— *Kara Ogushi, Online Forty-Niner*

"Jordan offers us an unadulterated peek through the curtains of reality...an intriguing exposé on all aspects of this misunderstood industry."
— *Alex Nye, UB*

"Anyone who might enjoy the dark humor of a satirical, behind-the-scenes look at a gentlemen's club...won't be disappointed by Stripped."
— *Dave Patrick, Spectator Magazine*

"[Stripped] is GREAT!"
— *Rick, GirlfriendX.com*

"There is stuff in there that shows you had intimate knowledge of what went on in the club...That is a very strong statement."
— *John Ralston, Face To Face*

"...the book is impossible to put down."
— *Doug French, Liberty Watch Magazine*

"...curt, straight to the point and no sugar coating his words, participation and actions. Mr. Jordan just told his story even when it meant showing his role in the business...I highly recommend the book."
— *Lisa, Florida*

"I know every word is true, and he does share a side with the reader that exposes a Vegas most people don't know."
— *BD, Las Vegas*

"I couldn't put it down...get it!"
— *Gin Rose*

"I couldn't put it down."
— *Sera, Los Angeles*

"I couldn't put it down."
— Ingrid Quenteros, *Las Vegas*

"...the perfect analogy for Las Vegas. All glitter and sparkle on the surface, hard-boiled and dark to the core... A Las Vegas primer that the city elders won't be putting on their tourist web page."
— *Cormac Vaughn*

"Jordan is a really terrific writer—the Henry Rollins of the strip bar world, all the more engaging because the skill and sensitivity is unexpected in a 6 foot 200 pound dude who kicks ass for a living. He's a great storyteller, has an intuitive BS detector that makes him a great truth-teller, and has a genuine empathy, understanding and nuanced appreciation for many of life's misfits who populate his books. Plus the stories are terrific! I read this in one sitting."

— Jonny Bowden, *PhD, CNS author of "Living the Low Carb Life: Choosing the diet that's right for you from Atkins to Zone" (Sterling 2004). Co-host of "The New You Show," KLLI Dallas.*

# STRIPPED

Twenty Years of Secrets From Inside the Strip Club

*A satirical parody.*

by
Brent Kenton Jordan

Satsu Multimedia Press

Stripped

ISBN 0-9703441-2-0

4th. Edition

Printed in the United States by Morris Publishing
3212 East Highway 30
Kearney, NE  68847
1-800-650-7888

For all those
who could not speak
for themselves.

Reality is for those
with no imagination.

"You can find meanness in the least of creatures, but
when God made man the devil was at his elbow."
— Cormac McCarthy, Blood Meridian

## PUBLISHER'S NOTE:

I do not believe a word of this story, not literally in any case. I do not believe it, because it seems inconceivable to me, that these situations, these acts, these characters, are real, that these events could have actually taken place—are taking place, now, at this moment, as I write this—simply inconceivable. How could there be so much ignorance, racism, violence, sex, corruption, greed...stupidity...? How this could continue to exist—at this time, in this country—is beyond my comprehension.

I read *Stripped*, and passed it around the office for feedback in a attempt to determine exactly what it was I was dealing with. The conclusion we drew seemed obvious: this was satire. The account of this man's twenty years as a strip club bouncer, was satire; a parody. The realization made me feel a little better about humanity. Then, I met the author.

The author/publisher relationship is often tenuous at best. One is greatly dependent upon the other: A publisher needs writers for their product, and a writer without a publisher has little chance of having his work broadly recognized. Though mutually dependent, the relationship is not always cohesive. I have no doubt that some of the greatest literary works in history are gathering dust in a desk drawer because of incompatibly between an author and a publisher.

When I first met Mr Jordan, the author of *Stripped*, I was instantly hurled into an author/publisher relationship unlike any I had ever experienced before.

"Brilliant satire," I said, rising to greet Mr. Jordan as he entered my office. I reached out my hand in greeting, and was left standing there, unreturned handshake extended, the smile withering on my face.

Mr. Jordan paused, glanced slightly around the room, as if insuring I was addressing him, then smiled an inside-joke sort of smile—half swallowed, half mocking—and finally shook my offered hand. "Okay," was all he said.

"Okay." What did that mean?

The remainder of the meeting went much the same, with my teetering off-balance, unsure.

I did ask for definitive confirmation of my satire notion, but all I received in return was an amused grin, and the assurance that all the stories herein were indeed his stories.

Mr. Jordan, though not as large as I had originally imagined (not more than 6'1", 210 pounds), displayed an overwhelming physical presence—an air. I wasn't scared, mind you, but the word comfortable, also does not come to mind. (I can't say I cared much for the way he called me "sir," either.)

I felt it necessary to clarify this, lest some readers misunderstand the nature of this work. *Stripped* is satire. It is a parody of a life and of an industry. At least I pray it is.

**Satire;**

1. A literary work in which vices, follies, stupidities, abuses, etc. are held up to ridicule and contempt.
    - *Websters Dictionary*


2. A legal G-string, a thin floss of lawsuit avoiding terminology.
    - *Scott Dickensheets*

*"There he goes. One of God's own prototypes.
Some kind of high powered mutant never even considered for
mass production. Too weird to live, and too rare to die."
- Hunter S. Thompson*

# THE GREATEST JOB IN THE WORLD

*B*lood pooled slowly, turning the concrete blackish-crimson under the flickering neon lights. A man's pain-filled face was pressed firmly into the center of the expanding viscous pool. His nose and mouth—crushed and ruined—seeped freely. His hair was matted with blood where the skin burst over his skull from the initial impact with the unforgiving blacktop. His breathing, labored and forced, came in raspy, unsatisfying gasps. He was pinned—immobile—to the ground by the heavy knee that pressed unrelentingly into the back of his neck. His ears rang with the buzzing hum that originated from somewhere deep inside his head, and further off he heard a voice—now suddenly close to his ear.

"If you bleed on my boots, I'll kill you."

The words only served to bring panic to what was left of the man's consciousness. Bile rose in his throat, lurching at the back of his broken teeth. He wanted to cry. He would have puked if the pressure on his neck wasn't crushing off its exit.

White noise filled his head, increasing...louder...all encompassing—nauseating dizziness—creeping blackness....

The last thing the man heard before he lost consciousness, sounded so familiar; something from his immediate past that now seemed like several lifetimes ago.

"Gentlemen. Welcome to Cheetahs."

## CHEETAHS TOPLESS CLUB, LAS VEGAS:

The neck under my knee belonged to a man who had been having, I am sure, what he considered to be a great time: the company of a strikingly beautiful young woman in the VIP room, nude but for a g-string and a pair of ridiculously high heels; tan legs, nineteen-year-old breasts, flawless skin—firm and smooth as spun silk over the finest porcelain. Lap dances until the wheels come off. Nothing wrong with that. What's not to enjoy? I could appreciate all that myself. A great time, and he had been having it, right up until it came time to pay.

It's something that never ceases to amaze me; if you received the service, pay for the service. This is not a trick. I am fairly certain the unfortunate gentleman had been thinking along the same lines thousands of ill-informed individuals have thought before him: "So I short her for a few dances. I already got the dances. What are they going to do, take them back, repossess them like a leased car? I'm ready to leave anyway. So they kick me out. What's the worst that could happen?"

What's the worst that could happen? Now he has an

inkling. That is why I am here. It is what I do. It's pretty much all I do. I am a bouncer in a titty bar in Las Vegas. What did you really think was going to happen?

Cheetahs Topless Club, established 1991, and I've been there from the beginning. I've seen every single employee of this place come and go; every manager, DJ, bartender, entertainer...everyone except the owner: that pissy son of a bitch with the ego from hell.

The customer was handcuffed and attended to by another bouncer. It really hadn't been much of an incident. I had applied the original choke-hold while his half-dozen or so friends watched in stunned, disbelieving horror. Then it was just dog-pile on the unlucky customer. Seven bored bouncers and one roid-raged manager, and that was pretty much all she wrote.

The situation was handled. I went back inside.

Tessa was waiting for me with a twenty-dollar bill, and a pair of soft lips.

"Thank you," she purred in my ear. Her hand with the twenty went in my pocket, and her lips moistened my cheek with a soft kiss. She let her manicured nails trace gently over my chest in way of further payment, and I gave her a brief hug, and copped a cheap feel in acknowledgment.

I watched Tessa as she turned to leave, we all did, me and the crowd of men who had gathered to witness the beating the club bouncers had just doled out.

"Damn, man, you've got the greatest job in the world," the twentysomething club kid with the perfect clothes, hair, tan, look, said to me as we watched Tessa disappear into the crowd.

"Yes I do," I agreed, then elaborated; "I'm surrounded by a hundred and fifty stunningly beautiful, naked young women who pay me copious amounts of money to watch them take their clothes off, and every once in a while, I get to slap the piss out of some moron who desperately needs it. What more could a man ask for?" I took a moment to reflect on my job description. It was ludicrous, really. It was as if a group of drunk, horny felons had thought up my job one night at the local tavern.

"It's got to get old after awhile though, right?" The kid asked.

"You're kidding, right?" I scoffed in response. "The day I get tired of this shit is the day I put a bullet in my eye."

Susie Q, an exceptionally affectionate entertainer, was passing by, and I reached out and pulled her close. She responded out of trained habit, grinding her pelvis into mine, and moaning in mock pleasure. I whispered in her ear what I wanted her to say, and she generously obliged...as she always did.

"Brent's the best fuck I've ever had," she said loudly to the stunned club kid, then ad-libbed a lusty grab to my groin for emphasis. Susie Q strolled away, leaving the gullible kid gaped-mouthed.

I composed, and adjusted, myself the best I could and smiled at the kid. "You know, when I got into this business they told me I would get tired of it after awhile—get immune to it."

"How long have you been doing it?" He asked.

"About twenty years. I suppose it might get old after awhile, but not yet." I smiled.

"Jesus, I guess not." He gave me the same look they all give me when I lay that act on them: the "God-I-wish-I-were-you-only-not-so-old-or-ugly" look. "How do you get a job here?" He asked, only half-joking.

"Kill somebody," I replied, filling in the other half of the joke.

I left the kid standing there with his friends as I fought my way through the packed club to the restroom to scrub my hands. I didn't see any blood on me anywhere, but you could never be too sure. One of these days, some jerk I had beat down (with my luck, for a relatively minor infraction), would have the last laugh and wind up killing me with his HIV-riddled blood. It was a risk of which I had been abysmally aware since the mid-1980s, but then every job had its drawbacks. I scrubbed my hands, and looked at myself in the wall-sized restroom mirror.

Far too many years in the business, I thought. I had taken a job in 1984 with Pacers Strip Club in San Diego after I was released from the Army. I had taken the job, something most people do for the summer while they're waiting to graduate from college, and had turned it into a career.

I had just tipped over the back edge of forty years old; bald, tired, deep creases around my eyes from squinting against the cigarette smoke—the same smoke coating my lungs—my knees creaked, my back ached, my feet had gone flat...and still, every man I met wanted to be me, at least for a day. I stared into the mirror some more. It wouldn't be AIDS that got me, I decided. It would be lung cancer, and I had never smoked a cigarette in my life. Twenty years of secondhand smoke. That's what would get me.

If the envious kid had only known the truth, he no doubt would have been sorely disappointed. He surely had been thinking of the prodigious amount of wild, unbridled, freaky sex to which a man in my position must have access. I wonder myself on that particular irony a great deal. As a matter of fact, in my life, I have had sex with fewer women than a good-looking club kid like that has sex with in a few months' time. The truth is, I met my wife fifteen years ago, and I made a commitment. A man honors his commitments. This is simply a fact.

Your honor is the only thing that can not be taken from you: You can surrender it, give it away, abandon it, but it can not be taken from you. It is the only thing you possess that can not be taken. This fact makes honor more valuable than all worldly possessions or virtues combined. To abandon your honor seems the greatest crime a man could commit. I can not imagine giving that up for anything, much less for a few hours of passion: Just another hard earned lesson from the strip club.

Does this attitude exclude me from flirting, teasing, fantasizing, or copping a feel here and there? Give me a break. I'm still just a man, and as self-righteous as I am, I wouldn't even attempt to lie about that—not even to my wife.

The greatest job in the world? For me it is, but then I'm an over-sexed, money-grubbing egomaniac with violent tendencies, lost in a century not his own. I couldn't dream up a better job.

*"That the only purpose for which power can be rightfully exercised over any member of a civilized community, against his will, is to prevent harm to others. His own good, either physical or moral, is not a sufficient warrant."*
*- J.S. Mill,*

## US AND THEM

*Y*ou are either one of us, or one of them. For a strip club employee, that fact slaps us across the face nearly every day. Moreover, many times it feels as if it is us *against* them, or more accurately, them *against* us. You will seldom meet a strip club employee who has consciously chosen their profession to be ostracized, belittled, berated, judged, slandered and looked down upon.

If you make your living in the strip club industry, you are one of us. If you do not, you are one of them: It is that simple.

I wrote this book based more or less on this fact. It has always amused me to see Hollywood's, and the media in general's, take on strip clubs. By amused I mean in a furious, ranting, maniacal, kill-everything-I-can-get-my-hands-on sort of way.

It amazes me that individuals, far more intelligent and educated than myself, can not see the sheer bewildering ludicrousness of the media's take on strippers, and the strip club industry.

I read articles, books, see movies, hear otherwise intelligent conversations by learned individuals, professing a knowledge of the industry, as if they have any way or means to back up that assumed knowledge. I've said it before and I'll continue saying it until the stars burn out of the sky: "You think you know what goes on in here? You don't have a clue."

It is maddening for me to read an account of a author's "expose" of strip clubs, put forth as if he had any true knowledge whatsoever of the subject on which he is postulating. What matter is it if a author spends a day, a year, ten years, a thousand years..., in a strip club, interviewing, listening, observing? He is still one of "them." What does he truly know at the end of all that research? I contend, nothing; nothing that those strip club employees did not want him to know; nothing that they did not put forth for their own motivations and for their own cause. An author will readily claim that men in these places are conned and coerced and worse, but not him, of course. He is the one who has been told the unadulterated truth. I liken it to listening to a lap dance patron claim, "I think she really likes me."

What makes an author imagine that what he sees and hears is anything but illusion and fantasy? Why would it be any other way? The entire industry is illusion and fantasy. It is why men come to us; for fantasy (certainly not reality. Who would want to hear about how fat, pathetic, and smelly they are?).

We in the strip club industry alter the truth into fantasy for a living. It is how we survive. Is anyone so arrogant to believe they can cut through that fantasy from the outside? That reasoning is akin to a strip club bouncer taking a couple political science courses at the local community college, interviewing a city councilman or two, and then having the audacity to write a book on political corruption. Ludicrous? Yes! And now you are beginning to see.

No matter what the circumstances—husband, wife, confidant, weekend employee...—you are either one of us, or one of them, and no matter how intelligent, or savvy, or how many hours are spent in the strip club, you will remain one or the other.

The saying goes, "before you criticize me, walk a mile in my shoes." Am I claiming you have to work in the strip club industry to truly know the strip club industry? I am claiming much more than that. My contention is this; not only must you work in the industry, but you must feel that it is your only real choice in life—the only means you have of supporting yourself or your family. You must work in the industry, not out of curiosity, or for frivolous income, but for your very survival. You must work in the industry far past the time you feel you can not bear to do it one more moment. Only then do you become one of us, and your opinions and insight on the business become valid.

I do realize that the vast majority of you have no interest in being one of "us," and if asked, you would claim you would rather gouge your own eyes out than work in the strip club industry, and that is fine. I truly appreciate your point of view. There are many professions I feel the same way about. However, before you feel free to profess knowledge of strippers, strip clubs, or the strip club industry, ask yourself one question: are you one of us, or one of them?

*"Nothing exists except atoms and empty space;*
*everything else is opinion".*
*- Democritus*

*"In America sex is an obsession,*
*in other parts of the world it is a fact."*
*- Marlene Dietrich*

## SEX

"Sex," her hot breath poured the word into his ear. "God I love it; on top of a man, the way I'm sitting on top of you right now. Feeling you inside me, filling me up," she breathed heavily. She let her soft lips caress his stubbled cheek as she adjusted herself on his lap, keeping her pelvis rotating ever so slightly to her own unheard tune, pausing only when his fluttering breath told her he was too close.

He reached to touch her thighs again, her skin velvety smooth, like hot, heavy cream poured over an impossibly firm bolt of silken fabric.

Again her hands caught his and gently pressed them back down to his sides. He had been allowed only a fleeting trailing over that breathtaking skin. He adjusted himself in his seat, hoping for any relief from the tension in his groin that seemed to suffocate him in the most pleasurable way. She was so light on top of him; petite, tiny, impossibly small. A single thrust would finish him...but not yet. She would not allow it. He could feel her heart beat in her chest, the light rhythmic pulsing against his cheek now—so soft, so delicate. He could feel his own pulse thumping against his groin. She had to feel it too.

Her smell was like the fondest memory from the favorite summer of his youth; young, sweet, warm. He wanted to breath her in, but he could barely breathe at all for the hot knot in his throat, and his shuttering, shallow breath (so close...so close...).

She held his face in her hands and forced him to look into her eyes; unfathomably beautiful, impossibly deep, painfully intense. Her eyes looked into his and he knew he was the only man on Earth—the only real man.

Her lips brushed his ear, her hot breath penetrating him. "Do you want another?"

Do you want another? He was brought back from the brink, suddenly aware of his surroundings.

The ear-piercing music had paused, the disc jockey was rambling another inane and redundant segue, and the droning noise of the club thundered around them. The lap dance was over, but the ATM was full and waiting, and he had all night.

****

## LAP DANCING

Is a lap dance sex? It certainly would not be by former President Bill Clinton's definition. Is it foreplay? Only when it is fulfilled, which it won't be. To the crude it is a zipless fuck. To the city council it's a (revenue-generating) stance. To the nonbelievers, it's a waste of money.

I can see the point of view of the first two, though I certainly don't agree, but not the latter: A waste of money? Never. I have spent much more money doing things I enjoyed a whole lot less.

Where else in this world can you get a strikingly beautiful twenty-year-old woman to perform nearly naked on your lap, without the fear of committing an illegal act, for a paltry twenty dollars? Think about it. For twenty dollars, about a third of the price to enter a theme park, you get a mind-blowing, erotic, adrenaline-pumping, bring-a-smile-to-my-face-for-weeks-to-come, beautiful experience. Twenty dollars! I can always earn another twenty dollars. I've paid more than that to have a kid park my car. When is the next time I'm going to have a chance to have a drop-dead gorgeous twenty-year-old on my lap, treating me like a God?

Is a lap dance a fantasy? Yes, without a doubt. But then why do we go to theme parks, the movies, watch mindless sitcoms, read novels, or any of the other countless methods we use to escape reality for a moment? It is a fantasy. A beautiful, harmless, stimulating, awe-inspiring fantasy, and it can all be yours for a mere twenty dollars.

But is it sex?

Don't kid yourself, it is not sex, not to her anyway, not in any way, shape or form. No matter what she tells you, no matter how she moans, or how her eyes roll back in ecstasy, or how you feel her quiver under your touch, it is not sex—not to her. To her it is a job. She is an actor; you are her audience. She no more gets off grinding on your lap than Harrison Ford found the Ark of the

Covenant.

Don't be to dismal about the seeming inequity of the encounter. She is fulfilling your fantasy and your physical need to be touched. You are offering her, in trade, what she needs most from you: cash.

A lap dance basically would be an even and fair trade of services for compensation except for one inevitable, nagging obstacle. The vast majority of men, for whatever reason, insist on taking the event to an unnecessary, obnoxious and asinine conclusion: "What is it going to take to get you to come home with me?"

Be it a lack of maturity in sexual matters, society-imposed expectations on how he is supposed to act in these situations, or possibly, sheer stupidity, I have no idea. Whatever the case, the unwelcome groping and ignorant comments and suggestions that spew from the average man receiving a lap dance, have wounded many of these young women in their soul to such a degree that it is a wonder they can carry on sexual relations with men at all.

It is little wonder that so many topless entertainers eventually explore their bisexual options.

## BISEXUALITY

A woman having sexual encounters with another woman. Do you find that strange, erotic, unnatural, exciting, disgusting?

In truth, I have never met a woman—in any environment—who under the proper circumstances, is *not* bisexual. You can attribute my statement to my environment if you wish, but if you open your eyes to the world around you, to women in business, college, the clergy...you will find it is true, and who can blame them? I am astounded every day that women, for whatever reason, would even consider having sex with males of the species. I am eternally grateful that they do (I don't like my remaining options), but in truth, I do have trouble understanding it.

Look at it this way: On one side you have a hairy, smelly, inconsiderate, poor-mannered slob with muted feelings, and a near-total lack of understanding of the female psyche (and body). On the other, you have a soft, considerate, caring, mirror image from which to reflect hopes, and dreams and concerns: erotically responsive and knowing in the matters of the female body. It's not exactly a toss-up if you ask me.

What does a man offer that a woman cannot? Procreation? You got me there. Procreation: an act that inevitably results in eighteen years of anger, frustration and exhaustion. A penis? Nothing a woman can't buy for a few dollars at her local adult toy shop, and in a variety of nonabusive, nonjudgemental colors and sizes at that.

Exotic entertainers turn to other women for love for even more specific and easily identifiable reasons than nonentertainers: because the men they entertain drive them to it. An exotic entertainer performs dozens of lap dances each night for men who callously grope and utter unwelcome inferences and degrading statements; men who are disrespectful in every word and action; men who go out of their way to be rude, obnoxious and revolting. A hardened, mature woman would be repulsed. A teenage entertainer, still developing in her perceptions, can be mortified.

A kinder, gentler reason women have sex with other women requires very little imagination. In a business based on erotic beauty, it is little wonder that an exotic entertainer might find another exotic entertainer sexually attractive. Similar look, emotions and philosophy earn mutual admiration among women who work so closely together. Familiarity with the human form, an elevated comfort with nudity and sexuality, a camaraderie in choosing to live on the fringe of society—all valid explanations. There may be nothing more sexually fulfilling than a partner who truly cares about and understands your fears, hopes, dreams and needs. And then there is just the sheer beauty of a woman.

To illustrate, imagine yourself in a room with Salma Hayek, Angelina Jolie, Adriana Lima, Jessica Simpson...(insert your favorite female here). Now imagine a beautiful young topless entertainer is asked to choose which one of you she would like to take to bed. It would be an unfathomably egotistical individual who could imagine *he* would be chosen first.

Lesbians, women who choose not to have sex with men under any circumstances, are nearly as rare in the strip club business as women who claim to be purely heterosexual. Lesbians are not made, but born. Sexual preference is inherent, God given, if you will. A lesbian is no more outstanding or unusual in society than a gay male. A lesbian, in the topless club industry, is only rare in that it must be immeasurably difficult for a woman, who finds no man sexually attractive, in any way, shape or form, to tolerate the demands put on exotic entertainers on a daily basis. Imagine yourself (heterosexual male) provocatively rubbing yourself on another heterosexual man's body for twenty dollars. Get it? (Not a pretty image.)

## GROUP SEX

Group sex—threesomes, moresomes, orgies: every man's fantasy. Two, three, four beautiful women exploring your body and each other's. Multiple hands, mouths, tongues, breasts.... Countless women intertwined around you and each other. A sea of steamy flesh, sweat-slicked bodies insatiable in their appetites, uninhibited, unrepressed, open to every concept, every suggestion, every possibility.... Be careful what you wish for.

Most topless club employees (entertainers and male employees alike) have engaged in threesomes or group sex. For the women it was probably a matter of curiosity, an openness to new experiences: the theory that if one is great, more must be better. For the men, well, honestly, most men rarely need a reason to have sex, but simply an opportunity.

If you are male and you work in a topless club, at one time or another you will probably date someone you work with. Chances are she is having sexual relations with at least one other entertainer. Odds are you will find yourself (in bed) between the two of them eventually. Is this a bad thing? Not at all, but be prepared. A man with two women is always the outsider, the stranger, the one disconnected by matter of gender if nothing else. If the combination was generated for you (as a gift, so to speak), you will find yourself in the midst of an experience that will make you smile in remembrance for the rest of your life. However, unless you are the most self-centered and selfish man ever conceived, the grouping eventually will turn to a more equitable paring, and you may find yourself, literally, the odd man out.

If you are open to the experience, simply being witness to two women making love can be the most erotic experience of your life. There is something awe inspiring about watching two beautiful women share a tender kiss or an erotic embrace. It is like witnessing a once-in-a-lifetime sunset, or a one-of-a-kind work of art.

Would I recommend engaging in sex with more than one woman? If you are an exceptionally strong-minded individual with an overabundance of confidence—or ultimately selfish—by all means, yes. In your life you may never find a more sexually stimulating experience outside of intercourse with the one you love. Otherwise, keep the group sex in the realm of unfulfilled fantasy, and spare your fragile ego a beating from which it may never recover.

## TOPLESS CLUB EMPLOYEES

Do the male employees (bouncers, managers, bartenders, DJ's) of a topless club get laid a lot? Yes, but it may not be for the reasons you think.

The typical layman thinks that strippers are promiscuous sluts, quick to jump into bed with anyone at any time. If this notion has ever crossed your mind, you should check yourself, because your ignorance is showing.

Stop and think about it: A topless entertainer who has been in the business for more than a week has heard every line, been propositioned from every angle, been lied to, promised, begged and coerced for sex in every manner imaginable. Do you really think you have anything new or original to add to what she has already heard, and rejected? Furthermore, an entertainer in a strip club is at work. She is not there to meet men, she is there to make a living. You are partying; she is working. It is far easier to pick up a woman at a dance club or regular bar than a strip club. The women at dance clubs and other bars are there to have a good time, and many times that means to meet people, men, maybe you. The women at a strip club are working (there may be a theme developing here). The number three complaint I have heard from topless entertainers over the years (behind, "my feet hurt" and "I'm not making any money tonight,") may well be, "This guy keeps asking me out. What does he think, I'm here to party?"

Keep in mind, a beautiful, hard-bodied twenty-year-old generally doesn't have that much trouble meeting men. She doesn't have to pay exorbitant amounts to the house for the privilege of getting undressed in a room full of drunks so she can find a date.

So why would it seem so easy for me, an aging, below-average-looking bouncer, to take a girl home from the strip club when I just stated it was nearly impossible to do so? In truth, it's just a matter of playing the odds.

I work with 150 girls per night. Possibly half of them do not find me sexually revolting, leaving 75 girls. Maybe half of those 75 are not dating anyone, or are having trouble with their significant others at the moment, leaving about 37 girls. Half of those 37 may actually like me well enough to consider going out with me, and half of that half I might be able to wear down with my banter. Add to that the fact these are people I work around every day, and have built relationships with—the same as in your office or workplace. Office romance happens. My office just happens to be a strip club.

The truth is, any man who works around 150 girls a night as their protector, confidant, authority figure, etc., can play the odds and find one woman who will take pity on him and join him in his bed. (Besides, my ego would never allow me any other belief.)

*"Mysteries made public become cheap and things profaned*
*lose their grace, therefore, cast not pearls before swine,*
*nor make a bed a of roses for an ass".*
*- Christian Rosencreutz*

## OF BOYFRIENDS AND FEMINISM

"*G*od, my boyfriend's the biggest asshole," the beautiful young woman pouted, her face still flushed from her recent encounter with the aforementioned individual. "I can't get hold of him for two hours, then he shows up down here and takes everything I made tonight so he can go out gambling. Now he's going to complain that we don't have any milk for his cereal in the morning."

"Yep," I replied. I had heard the same story a million times over the past twenty years, and "Yep" was about all the more emotion or compassion I could generate these days.

"God, I wish he would just leave," she said, her eyes welling. She was on the verge of tears as she pushed off the wall and sulked back into the room of waiting patrons.

\*\*\*\*

Years ago, in the infancy of my topless club career, I would have pursued the subject with her, trying to lead her to the seemingly obvious solution.

What does he do for a living?

Nothing.

He doesn't work?

No.

So you support him.

Yes.

You bought him that car he drives.

Yes.

And that big boat he takes out to the lake on weekends.

Yes.

And his clothes.

Yes.

All that gold he wears, and his dental work, and the dope he is continually high on....

Yes.

So why don't you just get rid of him and find someone who treats you like you deserve? You are young, ungodly beautiful...any man on the planet would kill to go out with you. You have your pick of men. You can go out with anyone you want. What do you need him for?

That's what I would have said, back in the days before I knew better. Back when I was in the habit of giving lousy advice.

An old joke: What does a stripper do with her asshole before she goes to work?

Answer: She drops him off at band practice.

Of course that joke was more appropriate back in

the 1980's when white trailer trash, Camaro-lovin', long-haired, dope-smokin', air guitar-playin' losers were about the worst an exotic entertainer could do.

Now, thanks to MTV or J.Lo or whatever godawful entity started the effect, exotic entertainers have found a much lower rung on the ladder with which to punish themselves—Pimps.

They aren't real pimps, or course, not in the traditional meaning of the word. They are wannabe pimps, by their own admission and title. Pimp is something they aspire to.

Who would voluntarily claim to be a pimp? You'd be surprised. I once, in a TV interview, heard a famous pop-star entrepreneur refer to himself, and his four-year-old son, as pimps. I have no idea what that means. The guy is a genius: An actor, performance artist, clothing magnate, multimillionaire...pimp? I do know that a good part of an entire generation of black men, and those who wish they were born black, have adopted the title to describe themselves and their attitude. I do understand the traditional definition of a pimp, and I can't imagine a lower or more despicable life form—except possibly for one who idolizes that life form. I don't get it. I don't think I want to. It is simply an observation.

I also know that an alarming number of young, beautiful white girls (I haven't met a black woman yet who would have a thing to do with them) have adopted these pimps as yet one more wall between themselves and society.

What sort of man (exceedingly loose definition of the title) would allow a twenty-year-old girl to support him without raising a finger to help? Rhetorical: a pimp, I suppose.

Why do exotic entertainers choose the men they do? Because they can, is the short answer. A common thread among many entertainers is fiercely independent natures and tendencies toward expedience. Many will choose to date below their station; that is, their elite physical beauty and income level. Often, it is simply more expedient to rent a mate than to cultivate one (at least while they are in the business).

Imagine you are an exotic entertainer for a moment. You are twenty years old, have a high school diploma, and are taking home eighty thousand dollars cash per year. Men your age are between their first job at McDonald's and their second job at Circuit City where, with commission, they will take home a whopping twenty thousand dollars this year. A twenty-year-old man working at Circuit City rarely is totally comfortable with his girlfriend taking her clothes off in front of hundreds of men each night, much less earning four times the money he does. Older men, who might not be intimidated by her comfort with nudity and her income level, generally have little in common intellectually, spiritually, recreationally, or sexually with anyone at the age of twenty. Where does that leave our entertainer?

Her choices are to try to find a man with such high self-esteem that he is totally accepting of a woman for who she is, and is not intimidated by her displays of nudity and high, if sporadic and temporary income (good luck), or, a man with such little self-worth that he is simply glad to have someone to take care of him, and not only support him financially, but buy into his half-baked, never-to-be-realized life dreams as well.

This is why exotic entertainers tend to gravitate toward the men they do, and simply purchase a boyfriend. Where is he going to go? Does he think he could ever do better than a strikingly beautiful young woman pulling down extraordinary money? And if he does leave, she can always find another just like him tomorrow.

This attitude may make exotic entertainers the ultimate feminists.

The ultimate feminists! Are you insane? How can you seriously equate being a stripper with being a feminist? I can nearly hear you screaming now.

First, being a stripper is a job. It is not a race, ideal or political stance: It's a job. It is what she does, not who she is. Moreover, consider the basic attributes of feminism; being independent, not being held down by convention, making your own way in life, living outside the status quo and expressing yourself in any way you see fit. These are also the attributes of the exotic entertainer. An exotic entertainer makes her living manipulating men and their systems. They exploit a man's insecurities and weaknesses like few others can. If you do not consider that feminism, you should check your understanding of the term again.

In the preceding example, an exotic entertainer puts herself, not on level with, but above the most powerful of men. She uses his own tactics of control and exploitation to take advantage over the perceived creators of such thought.

If you still scoff at the notion of strippers being the ultimate feminists, at least consider this: In the case of two women—any two women—what makes one's opinion more valid than the other's? If you are a feminist and you answered that a stripper cannot have a valid opinion, you have just done more damage to your cause than the most vile of chauvinists.

I had the opportunity to speak with two extremely successful businesswomen outside Cheetahs one night. They had visited the club with their company CEO and a high-profile client. The CEO had chosen the strip club to entertain his client in celebration of a recent deal. The two businesswomen were drug along as part of the celebration. After an hour or two, the two women had begged off and left the CEO and client to their own devices. The two women were waiting for a taxi outside as I overheard their conversation and interjected my own opinions on the subject:

"I hate coming to these places," one woman complained.

"I know, it's like you can't sign a deal without tits in your face," the other agreed.

Both women were fortyish, and very attractive with their sharp business suits and powerful demeanor.

"You got the deal signed?" I asked from where I had been standing at the valet stand behind them.

The women looked at me appraisingly—not kindly—and favored me with a condescending tone and a brief response, "Yes, we did."

"And you're not going to stay and celebrate?" I asked.

"Why, so I can watch my boss and this billion-dollar client go all goo-goo over some stripper?" Both women turned their backs on me. The conversation was over as far as they were concerned.

"Was it a tough sale?" I probed.

Both women looked back to the front door of the club to be sure we were alone before they answered. "The guy's a real hard-assed prick, actually. One of the richest men in the world and he wants to screw you for every dime."

"But he's in there emptying his wallet for some stripper, right?" My observation might as well have been salty lemon juice in a paper cut considering the venomous look I received.

"She's probably going to make my entire commission off the guy," one of the women scoffed sourly.

"And that doesn't tell you anything?" I queried.

"Like what?" She demanded. "Maybe I should toss my business degree and become a stripper?"

"Well, as attractive as you both are, and as much as I would love to see you take your clothes off, that wasn't my point." They may have blushed. It was cute. "Look," I said, "I just met you and already I'm trying to think of a way to get you into bed." I was cautious of a violent reaction as I illustrated my point. "Do you know why?"

"Because you're a man," one woman answered. She was quick. And this time I was sure she was blushing.

"That's exactly right," I conceded, "and so is your boss, and most of your clients I imagine. As much as they respect your intellect and your business skills, they are still men, which means they still, somewhere in the back of their puny, primitive minds, want to take you to bed."

"So there's a news flash. I'm not going to sleep with

every client just for a sale." The two women feigned disgust with me, and the perceived inference, but they were both sharp enough to know that's not what I was getting at.

"Have either of you ever read Musashi's 'Book of Five Rings'?" I asked.

"In college. It was required for a business course," one replied. "So?"

"Do you remember a passage that stated, 'To die with a weapon yet undrawn is to die uselessly'?" Neither woman remembered the passage, but they gave me the benefit of the doubt. "It means use all your weapons to defeat your opponent. All your weapons." The women looked thoughtful. I smiled. "While you are playing down your inherent advantage of the fact you are attractive women, and only using your intelligence and business skills, you are fighting with only half your weapons."

"He's got a point," one woman begrudgingly admitted to the other.

"Blind them with you sexuality, dazzle them with your brilliance, overwhelm them with all your weapons," I concluded.

It was about then that their taxi pulled up, but they left with a thoughtful look on their brows and, I like to think, a newfound respect for their own attributes.

So, you think you are man enough to date exotic entertainers—the ultimate feminists? If you are strong enough to handle the unique situation, you have my respect. Most men aren't. As for myself, I couldn't imagine a relationship with any other sort.

*"Senatus Populusque Romanus" (Better we begin our discourse now with swords than our tongues.")*
*- Otto I*

*"Ultima ratio regnum" - (The Last Argument of Kings)*
*- inscription on artillery forged under rule of Louis XIV*

# VIOLENCE

"*Y*ou can't do that!"

"Can't or shouldn't?" I asked sardonically. "I think you are getting those two confused."

He struggled against my grip, but he wasn't going anywhere, not until we said so, anyway. I leaned a little harder on the wrist lock/pain compliance hold until the man arched his back and grimaced in pain. Big Mike had the man by the other arm, and Big John was standing behind him casually gripping a handful of the unfortunate fellow's hair.

We were in no hurry. We would get him up and out when wc were good and ready. Until then, the surrounding customers could enjoy the show, and consider the proper attitude with which to approach all dealings in a strip club.

Now, we were ready. We hefted the man to his feet and herded him out the side door like a lamb being led down the funnel ramp to the killing car. He struggled the best he could, which was considerable considering his size and bulk, but it was three on one, and any one of us, trained and sober, had a decided advantage.

Roughly out the side door he went, stumbling and tripping, barely able to keep his feet. When he turned, he was faced with three rather large, hostile individuals: three strip club bouncers.

Had he stopped to reflect on the facts, or had he been two drinks more sober, he probably could have saved himself the inevitable.

He was a big man, probably not accustomed to being handled the way in which we were handling him. He had probably played some football in college. He was probably used to getting his way. Not tonight. The man rolled his thick neck through rubbery layers of fat, and squared off against the three of us, albeit from a good ten feet away.

"You know what?" He spat. "Fuck you guys. You're a bunch of fucking pussies. Three on one, you guys are a bunch of fucking faggots." His face was red with adrenaline and anger as he screamed the words at us. He was making it just too damn easy.

"Shoo," I taunted him, waving as I would at an annoying fly. "Go away, you little bitch, before this fag bends you over the hood of that car and fucks you in the ass."

"Fuck you, man, I'll fuck you in the ass. Just you and me, right now!" He waved me forward with the challenging words. I was always the popular one to call out; me, with my big mouth and relatively small stature.

I smiled, scoffed, and shook my head happily. Too easy, I thought. I smiled my biggest smile and laughed aloud. "You know, my six-year-old throws tantrums just like that...right before I spank him." As I spoke, Big Mike and Big John moved off to the sides just far enough to allow the furious man a thought of a shot at me. "Now, shoo, scram, get. Go home and tell your wife how you got punked out by some little fag."

That was all he could take. The alcohol, adrenaline, and his own ego got the best of him, and he rushed me—finally.

It was hard to say which happened first: if the big man had completed his third step toward me, or if Big Mike's haymaker caught him on the side of the head. In any case, it was even harder to say which of the three of us bouncers got in the most, or the most damaging, shots. The big man was beaten until all thoughts of resistance were hammered from him. In the end, he was curled in a tight fetal position, and our fists and feet were sore from the repeated impacts.

The inert figure was handcuffed and delivered to the police, along with three remarkably similar incident reports written by the three victims (we three bouncers) of the unprovoked attack by the violent, aggressive, intoxicated, irrational customer (henceforth to be referred to as suspect).

****

It would have served Mr. Suspect well to remember several obvious facts about his situation. Of course, retrospect is always far more clear a judge, but there were certainly enough indicators to have tempered the man's actions.

First, when you are in a topless bar in Las Vegas, it can be a lifesaver to remember that this is not California. The citizens of California have been conditioned to believe that "can't" and "shouldn't" are similes. They are not—not in a Vegas strip club. "Can't" drag you out of the bar for telling me to fuck off, would infer a physical inability. "Shouldn't," simply means the option I chose might not have been the most prudent option, and my actions might cause me grief in the long run. Think of it in terms of telling a speeding driver that he can't run you over as you are crossing the street in the crosswalk. What you mean is, he shouldn't hit you because you have the right of way. Of course, after you are splattered all over the street, what difference do semantics really make? So, now I have to write an incident report for the lawyers, and lie to the police again. You have still taken a beating.

Next, remember, professional bouncers are not going to "fight fair." The strip club is not a school yard or a boxing ring. The bouncers are there to maintain security, in the most expedient manner possible. They are not there to prove their manhood, or mettle, in a fight. They are working. That means if you only find yourself facing a three-on-one situation, consider yourself lucky. If you want a fair fight with a bouncer, wait until he is off work, then offer the challenge. I haven't met a professional bouncer yet who wouldn't jump at the opportunity to test his skill in a one-on-one street fight. I routinely informed disgruntled patrons the exact minute I would be off the clock. Oddly enough, in twenty years, I never had a single man accept my offer to meet for a "fair fight." (I have had many waiting on me with baseball bats, golf clubs, knives, guns—twice—and even a mason trowel once, but never a stand-up, squared-off fist fight.)

Finally, if you are thinking Rodney King-like, and expect a generous settlement from the establishment for the undeserved punishment you received at the hand of their employees, remember, this is not California (or Chicago, or Oregon, or New York...). Judges in Nevada have no special affinity for sex-offending thieves who molest defenseless girls, steal their money, and then try to fight their way out of a strip bar.

"What?" You say. "I didn't do any of that! All I did was tell a bouncer to fuck off when he asked me to stop being rude to the cocktail waitresses!" Odd, because that's not what it says in the three signed witness reports that were given to the police at the time of your arrest.

If it sounds like I am saying that three floor hosts (we are never called bouncers in court) would file false police reports, and lie under oath just to save their asses, I am. I did not write this account to make you feel better about the world, and humanity, and prove that justice prevails in the end. I know for a fact that it does not. I wrote this to tell the truth, and if you find it distasteful, I offer no apologies. It is still the truth.

The truth is, I have never seen a single incident report, of the many I have witnessed or invented, that told the unbiased truth. Actually, that is not as shocking a statement as it might at first seem. I would think every human past the age of two would know there are always three versions of the truth: my version, your version and what really happened. Unfortunately (for many patrons), of the thousands of incident reports I have penned over the years, it was only my version that mattered in the end.

Falsifying an incident report and altering the truth under oath is not as risky as it probably should be. Floor hosts are trained professionals working in an inherently hazardous environment. Customers under the influence of alcohol and drugs are the norm. Taking the word of a trained, sober professional, engaged in the duties of his job, over that of a drunk topless bar patron, is not a stretch. In addition, police and judges are not in the habit of biting the hand that feeds them. Topless clubs pay a lot of taxes, fund a lot of political campaigns, hand out a lot of free drinks, and are willing to cover a lot of indiscretion. Furthermore, wherever it is you are from (even if not California), your attorney probably does not have a license to practice in Nevada, which leaves you with local attorney options. You would be very lucky, almost lottery lucky, not to choose one who had a tie of some kind with the topless bar from which you are seeking restitution.

A beating in a strip club can be administered at almost any time for almost any reason; the entertainer whom you rejected took offense. The waitress or bartender who waited on you thought your toke (token = tip) was a bit on the light side. You gave the bouncer, with ten times the normal amount of synthetic testosterone in his blood, the wrong look. Your skin was too dark.... Like sex for the average man—for a topless bar bouncer—there doesn't so much need to be a reason to deliver of beating, as simply an opportunity. Argue with an entertainer, cocktail waitress, bartender, manager, DJ, or another customer, and you offer an opportunity. Have a complaint about the service, the lap dances, the lack of seating or the temperature of the room, and you offer an opportunity. Bring yourself to the attention of any employee in a less-than-positive light (read toke), and you open the door of opportunity. With that criteria, it seems there would be a beating administered every day. Exactly. Does that seem harsh? It is.

It has been estimated that I have been in over 8,000 physical confrontations in my 20 years as a strip club bouncer (an extremely conservative estimate, assuming just 1.75 per shift). I resist calling them fights. Most were just beatings. I am well trained and highly skilled as a fighter. The typical man is not prepared for the level of violence I bring to a fight. Besides, I could not afford to lose a fight. If I lost, someone in my charge could be hurt: Not on my watch.

Remember, in a strip club you are surrounded by people who work on the fringe of society, and can be very resentful of that fact. The entertainers resent your inferences. The cocktail servers resent your impatience and lack of gratitude. The bouncers resent your (greatly imagined) condescending nature. The managers resent having to work at all. The owner resents the exorbitant cost that is extracted by the local and federal governments to do business unmolested. There is a great deal of resentment and anger beneath the surface of a strip club. One must be cautious, and a little lucky, to avoid becoming the brunt of that anger.

If you would like to reduce your chances of receiving a beating while visiting a fine establishment such as Cheetahs—for example—you must become invisible, or better yet, revered.

An invisible customer is one who never complains. He purchases several cocktails, and tips for each. He sits on the stage and tips every entertainer who performs there, or buys dances from quiet, passive, sober entertainers. A customer, to remain invisible, must never argue under any circumstances. If a bouncer tells him to leave, the invisible customer doesn't ask why, he doesn't look for a reason, he doesn't try to explain that it is a case of mistaken identity—that he has done nothing wrong. The invisible customer never hesitates or looks over his shoulder on his way out the door to see if the bouncers are still behind him (the bouncers are, waiting for the customer to look back over his shoulder: an opportunity for a beating). The invisible customer never responds when an angry entertainer or cocktail waitress begins calling him names that would make a felon in Oakland lockup blush. An invisible customer never hesitates to give up his seat when the manager tells him he is sitting in a reserved table, the same table where he has been sitting for the past three hours. Even then, having done everything right, the invisible customer is still a potential victim of a beating. I have seen situations where an especially aggressive bouncer or manager has taken the invisible customers total compliance as an admission of guilt, and delivered a beating.

It isn't fair, it isn't right, it doesn't even make any sense. I never said it would. I simply said it's the truth.

Now, if you are thinking that maybe you, and your group, can beat the club's bouncers at their own game, you might want to think the notion all the way through. Certainly it is physically possible for a thirty-man bachelor party, all trained martial artists, barroom brawlers and former ball players, to succeed in a fight against the seven or eight bouncers and managers the club has on duty to resist you. It is possible; however, in my experience it is a bad bet and a very bad idea.

Keep in mind, even if you are able to best the bouncers in a fight, many male employees in a strip club carry guns, and have been waiting their entire lives for an excuse to use them. My recommendation: don't give them an excuse. Even if you and your friends don't wind up getting shot, you still have to try and escape after the fight. Did you take a cab, a limo, a bus, drive your own cars (with license plates)? Most topless clubs are not integrated into the finer neighborhoods. Take Cheetahs Las Vegas, for example. You have Interstate 15 behind you, the railroad tracks opposite (both well-insulated from foot traffic), and a couple of miles of industrial and retail in either direction. Where are you going to go? I have seen customers who have committed an infraction, and succeed in outrunning the bouncers, only to find themselves lost in the middle of nowhere.

I remember one incident when the bouncers didn't even bother chasing a fleet-footed customer who had run from the club after committing a beating-worthy act. We simply let him run, hailed ourselves a taxi, and chased the man until he couldn't run any farther. That gentleman may have taken a well-deserved beating from a carload of amused bouncers, but he was one of the lucky ones.

Another customer who was not lucky enough to be hunted down by the club's security force was mugged, beaten, robbed and left bleeding on the side of the road, without his shoes. The man hadn't had any money (the reason he had run from the club in the first place), and had been robbed by a group of street thugs, for his shoes.

One frightening episode I remember, was when we engaged in a bloody brawl with almost thirty off-duty sheriff deputies from another state—members of a bachelor party. There had been an argument at the front door about the cover charge—who had paid, who hadn't—and the cops had tried to bum rush the front door en masse. (generally a cop simply flashes his "gold card" (badge) to bypass the cover charge. In this case there had been some sort of confusion).

The bouncers started shoving, the cops shoved back, and it was on. After nearly everyone involved was bloodied and bruised, common sense (or fatigue) began to set in, and the combatants separated briefly. Some of the cops wanted to leave, cut their losses and call it a day, but the driver of the charter bus they had all come on had locked himself in the bus and refused to open the doors until the club gave him the okay. The bus driver wasn't about to be an accomplice, a getaway driver as it were, with his license-number printed all over the outside of his vehicle. The cops were stuck. Given the time, the cops might have prevailed in the fight, but then what? The cops couldn't try and walk back to their hotel, they barely knew where they were. They couldn't call for the local, on-duty police (try explaining that one to internal affairs back home). The incident ended when the club settled for payment of twenty dollars per head from the cops—for our trouble—and we gave the bus driver the okay to open the doors and haul his clients away.

Try and remember why you came to the topless bar

in the first place: the girls. You did not go to the strip joint to fight. You did not gather your friends from around the world, to Las Vegas, for a bachelor party, just to end up in jail, then in court. You went to the strip club for the only good reason there is to go to a strip club: the girls. Maybe the best advice I can give, is to always remember where you are, where you are not, and what your intentions were for being there in the first place.

I have witnessed enough people perform enough stupid, ignorant, nonsensical acts to last me a thousand lifetimes. I am haunted today, and forever, by the acts I have witnessed and have committed. If I never have to lay my hands on another human in anger, it will be far too soon. There will be a reckoning for me one day. I have amassed an overwhelming karmic debt that may never be repaid.

Then again, I have also used my gifts to defend those who could not defend themselves, and in the large scheme, who is to say which is worse and which is better.

For those who tell me, "Those who live by the sword shall die by the sword," I will reply, "and who would have it any other way?"

## INCIDENT REPORTS

An incident report, or voluntary statement, as the police like to call it (or, as I like to refer to it, a brilliant work of fiction), is used to prove, in a court of law, exactly how you, the customer, are solely responsible for any and all injuries and indignities you sustained while patronizing the strip club. The following is an example of an incident (what really happened) followed by the incident report given to police following the the incident (beating).

## THE INCIDENT:

A customer allowed an entertainer to perform two hundred dollars worth of lap dances in the VIP room. The customer only had one hundred forty dollars on him. When asked to get the rest of the money through the ATM machine, or a cash advance on his credit card, the customer refused. The manager, who was handling the situation, along with three bouncers, 'roid-raged and began beating the customer. The bouncers joined in, and the customer was choked, pummeled, and brutalized all the way out the door, and for several minutes in the parking lot. The customer was handcuffed, the police were called, and the beating slowed to the occasional slap or kick until the police arrived.

## THE (SAMPLE) INCIDENT REPORT:

*At approximately 1:20 A.M. Friday 13 June 2003, I was stationed at the back VIP room when I was alerted by several entertainers to a Suspect (Hispanic male, 25 years old, 5' 8", 160 lbs., Brown hair/eyes) who was attacking an Entertainer inside the VIP room. The Suspect was witnessed forcibly placing his right hand on the Entertainer's genital area in a sexual assault. The Entertainer was fighting and struggling against Suspect and calling for assis-*

*tance.*

*The Suspect was forcibly holding Entertainer and preventing her from escaping. When I arrived on scene, I asked the Suspect to release the Entertainer.*

*The Suspect refused and screamed; "Fuck you, you white devil! Get away from me or I'll kill you!" The Suspect continued to assault the Entertainer.*

*I assisted the Entertainer in escaping the Suspect, using the least amount of force necessary to secure the release of the Entertainer, by holding the Suspect's wrists while the Entertainer escaped.*

*I immediately released the Suspect as soon as the Entertainer was out of immediate danger.*

*The Suspect then grabbed an environmental weapon (beer bottle) in his right hand and stated to me: "I am going to kill you, white devil!" The Suspect stood and struck me with the weapon several times about the head and shoulders.*

*I defended myself to the best of my ability using the least amount of force necessary to ensure my safety, and the safety of the Suspect and surrounding customers and employees.*

*The Suspect continued to strike me about the head and shoulders with the weapon, and I was rendered semicon-*

*scious. Club security arrived to secure the Suspect, and after and extensive struggle, was able to disarm him.*
*The Suspect continued to fight and struggle and made several threats against our lives. The Suspect stated; "I am going to come back and shoot everyone here!" And, "I am going to firebomb this place and kill everyone." The Suspect was secured and restrained with handcuffs and was escorted outside using absolute minimal force.*

*Metro Police were called, and the Suspect was remanded to Police custody.*

*I may be seeking medical treatment for my injuries.*

*Signed and dated.*

This statement, combined with half a dozen other security statements along the same lines, in addition to the entertainer's statement about how the suspect had threatened to kidnap, rape and kill her, is enhanced with several customer claims that it went just that way (you might be surprised what the average regular customer will say for a free drink and a lap dance or two). This gentleman (suspect) finds himself in a world of hurt in a dispute over a few dollars. Sexual assault, assault with a deadly weapon, battery, terrorist threats, hate crime violence, and God knows what else.

My advice: Do you best to avoid confrontation at the strip club.

Because of the seemingly endless and imaginative ways customers find to take unnecessary beatings at strip clubs, I thought I would include the top six methods I have seen over the years—the most efficient, sure-fire ways—to get your ass kicked by a strip club bouncer.

TOP SIX LIST:
HOW TO REQUEST A BEATING AT A STRIP CLUB.

### 6) Don't leave the club when asked.

It doesn't matter why you were asked to leave. Do you really think the bouncer is going to change his mind, no matter how much you argue? Besides, why would you want to stay somewhere you are not wanted?

### 5) Threaten to speak with a manager.

If the bouncer is going to get in trouble for something he did or said to offend you anyway, he might as well give you a beating: As soon be shot for a lion as a lamb. If he makes the story good enough, he might even look justified.

### 4) Treat a cocktail waitress like an entertainer.

If a cocktail waitress wanted to be treated like a topless entertainer, she would be a topless entertainer. She wouldn't be fighting the crowd to lug your drink order across the room for that two dollar tip you are going to leave her.

### 3) Belittle a bouncer.

Go ahead, poke sticks at the lion. You would be amazed at the number of "two-beer-Rambo's" who like to speak down to and attempt to degrade and belittle a bouncer. That's just plain stupid if you ask me.

### 2) Don't pay for...

There is nothing a club owner will excuse more readily than a bouncer delivering a beating to a customer who refuses to pay for a lapdance or a cocktail: Titties and beer: the club's foundation. Mess with either at your own risk.

### 1) Piss off an entertainer.

A strip club doesn't exist without its entertainers. Bouncers, cocktail waitresses, bartenders, managers, barbacks, clean-up crew...the owner himself, could not earn their living without the entertainers. The club will keep them happy. Bet your life on it.

*"He that is of the opinion money will do everything may
well be suspected of doing everything for money."
- Benjamin Franklin*

*"Make money, money by fair means if you can,
if not, but any means money."
- Horace*

## MONEY

"*T*his sucks," the young woman pouted.

"What's the matter, baby?" The question automatically flowed from me in response to the standard entertainer's statement I hear maybe fifty times a night.

She plopped herself against my chest like a child in the midst of a tantrum. The young woman cuddled up close to me, working her head up under my chin until I could smell the freshness of her hair. She had been at work less than twenty minutes.

"The guys are so cheap tonight. Nobody has any money."

"I know, baby. It's the first of the month and everybody's got to pay their rent. I don't think there's anything in town this week either. The good conventions don't start for another month yet." There's always a reason.

"But I have to pay my rent too!" Now she was just whining, which would have been annoying coming from anyone less cute than the striking young woman who was trying to crawl in my shirt with me. "I need like twenty-two more dances."

I did a little quick math in my head and came up with four hundred forty dollars. "Is that all?" I hoped I didn't sound too sarcastic.

"I know," she acknowledged, "but my customer came in last night and I spent like three hours with him and he was being cheap."

"Oh, I'm sorry, baby. The cheap son of a bitch. How much did he give you?"

"Like twelve hundred, and he knows I have to make a double car payment this month, because I missed last month, because, remember, my sister was sick and I had to go home for..."

I lost everything after the first three words, and retreated to my dream-state of what I might do with twelve hundred dollars per day. Sometimes I wish I had been born a beautiful woman.

****

It still amazes me how much money goes down in a strip club, and how much we, the employees, take it for granted. Twelve hundred dollars. It was almost exactly double what I had been making, per month, when I first got into the business in 1984. "This sucks," and "he gave me twelve hundred dollars" generally wouldn't fit in the same thought, but I have known entertainers who have made that much in a single night, then bummed cab fare the next day. Easy come, easy go. The more you make, the more you spend. It's all relative. Take your pick of maxims, we in the business have a million of them.

Exactly how much money is spent just on the girls in an average night? A conservative formula might be as follows: Take one hundred seventy-five girls making an average of five hundred dollars, and you come up with eighty-seven thousand five hundred dollars—that's in one club, in one night, on one shift—and that's just the entertainers.

Keep in mind, I am getting these numbers from what I know of Cheetahs, and Cheetahs is not one of the bigger strip clubs in Las Vegas. These numbers truly are conservative.

Cheetahs, as of this writing, charges its entertainers sixty-five dollars per shift to work. (Each of the entertainers is an independent contractor. She must pay to work at the club. The cost to work goes up every year. When I started, the fee to work was five dollars.) One hundred seventy-five entertainers, times sixty-five dollars each, equals eleven thousand three hundred seventy-five dollars to the club. (These figures do not include the most recent fee of twenty-five dollars each, if the girl would like to be excluded from stage sets which cost her time, money and energy.)

There is a twenty-dollar cover charge at the door. On a Friday night shift (9 p.m. to 5 a.m.) approximately eighteen hundred customers pay the cover charge. Eighteen hundred customers times twenty dollars per head equals thirty-six thousand dollars.

Drink sales among all five registers on the 9-to-5 shift will total about twenty-five thousand dollars.

So, total income for Cheetahs on a Friday night

shift (by my reckoning) is about seventy-two thousand three hundred seventy-five dollars. The club is open three hundred sixty-three days per year, twenty-four hours per day.

Saturday night will total about the same as Friday, with Sunday through Thursday coming in at twenty to thirty percent less.

Least you believe only the club owner and entertainers are pulling it down in these joints, don't forget the management.

Each Cheetahs manager receives a salary of two hundred fifty to three hundred fifty dollars shift pay per day, paid in cash, daily. There are eleven managers for Cheetahs. (I know what you are thinking, eleven managers for three shifts? I will explain that amazing little club idiosyncrasy later in the Management chapter.) The real money for the managers comes from dividing up of the entertainer's work fee. Five dollars from the sixty-five-dollar shift fee each entertainers pays goes to the managers. The rest goes to the owner. On a shift where one hundred seventy-five entertainers pay the shift fee, a manager stands to make an extra eight hundred seventy-five dollars in addition to his shift pay—each day.

A good example is Mr. Blunt, Cheetahs' current (as of this writing) general manager. If this manager averages approximately eleven hundred seventy-five dollars per day, five days per week, this individual would take home about five thousand eight hundred seventy-five dollars per week, twenty-three thousand five hundred per month, and two hundred eighty-two thousand dollars per year—cash. I wonder what he claims on his tax returns?

It is no wonder that Cheetahs managers typically live in half million dollar homes, drive fifty thousand dollar SUV's, and have enough toys (jet skis, Harleys, boats, etc.) to open an RV rental shop. I won't begrudge management their income or life styles. After all, I have witnessed how they are forced to agonize over what to order for dinner at three in the morning when all the good restaurants are closed, or how hard it is to dodge the owner when he comes in, in a tirade, wanting to know why the 90 foot sign hasn't been turned on all night (it's hard to remember details when you have all the duties of a Cheetahs manager).

Am I bitter at all? Okay, maybe just a little.

As much as local government whines and postures about topless clubs, it would be hard to imagine an industry more beneficial to the local economy. Between the club owner, management, entertainers and other employees, literally millions of dollars are circulated each day in Las Vegas and other towns where exotic entertainment is tolerated. Unlike most other industries, strip club work means cash in hand—a lot of cash—and that cash is thrown back into goods and services as fast as it is collected. You can love the exotic entertainment business or hate it, but none can deny the profound impact it has on the local and national economy.

From a customer perspective, how much money is a lot of money? Again, "a lot" is a relative term.

To an entertainer who is uncomfortable taking home less than five hundred-plus per night, a five-dollar bill isn't going to raise her eyebrow. Likewise, a waitress delivering thirty dollars' worth of cocktails to your group, a five-spot probably won't get her rushing back through the packed club with a tray piled full with your next round. Remember, currently (as of this writing, and it changes quickly) a lap dance minimum is twenty dollars. Cocktails are six dollars and up. Cocktail waitresses are accustomed to making almost as much as the entertainers. Bartenders, twice that. You complain to the manager that you just dropped three hundred dollars in his club, and all he is thinking is that it isn't even a decent football parlay bet. On the other hand, you can hand a bouncer a twenty and he will find you a seat in the standing-room-only club in a matter of minutes. Write a song request on a twenty-dollar bill and hand it to the DJ and your favorite lap dance song will be playing within the hour. Slip a pair of twenties into the palm of the doorman and your party of four will suddenly appear on the guest list minus the cover charge and line.

If you are trying to impress someone in a topless club with your generosity, it gets a little tougher. Spending more than a grand on an entertainer generally will make a lasting impression (if you are not too rude; otherwise she will consider it what you owe her for your being difficult). Twenty will get you a table, but the most I have ever personally seen spent to get a party of nineteen seated was six hundred dollars. Twenty dollars will also get you past the hour wait to get into the VIP lounge, but c-notes are not at all uncommon.

Strip clubs are never cheap experiences, but they don't need to break you, either. A twenty here and there will make you a bona fide good guy, someone who always gets a seat and is overlooked when the nightly beatings are being dispensed. Buying two twenty-dollar lap dances in a row, toking the entertainer ten dollars on top and thanking her (and letting her get back to work without wasting too much of her time) will get you a pleasant smile and some nice conversation each time you come back.

So, bottom line, how much is a lot?

Here is an example of a lot of money: Each year, for a private party, on a Tuesday night, a certain Internet porn billionaire rents the club for four hours. The established price: thirty thousand dollars. This gentlemen also had a tendency to hand out hundred-dollar bills as if they are singles. As far as I know, a c-note is the smallest denomination he carries. That pretty much impresses everyone involved. Short of that, don't try to impress anyone, just know going in that you are going to spend enough money to support a family of four in Haiti for a year.

Here is a piece of advice that will keep everyone happy: If you can't afford it, don't go to the strip club.

*"Women who seek to be equal with men lack ambition."*
*- Timothy Leary*

*"Women prefer men who have something tender about them*
*— especially the legal kind."*
*- Kay Ingram*

## GIRLS, GIRLS, GIRLS

"*A*m I getting fat?" The nineteen-year-old Latin stunner turned her back to me and pulled up her skirt, exposing her tanned Lopez-esque backside and tiny floss g-string.

"Looks good from here," I said. That's me, the master of understatement.

"Do you think I need bigger tits?" She asked, turning back around to face me and cupping both her breasts in her hands, giving them an appraising squeeze and light massage.

"Breasts don't get any nicer," I assured her. "Trust me, I'm a professional."

"I was thinking about getting a tit job."

"Don't you dare," I blurted. She released her breasts and backed into me and pulled my arms around her. I tried to find a place for my hands that wouldn't be considered copping a feel. I wasn't entirely successful.

"That guy over there said my butt was too big and

my tits were too small."

"Too small for what?" I wondered aloud.

"He said he would buy a dance if I had bigger tits."

I probably would have pushed off the wall then and gone over to the offending customer, pulled a random piece of his body off with my bare hands, and fed it to him, but by then the young woman—who had her butt nestled into my stiffening crotch—had interlaced her fingers in mine and was massaging her breasts again, this time with both our hands. Hey, I could always dole out the needed beating later. Right now I was busy, consoling.

"Fuck that fat piece of shit!" I spat. "His opinion means nothing. Less than nothing. He doesn't count. He's not even real." I could feel a rant coming on. It genuinely annoyed me when customers did that. "That fat ass piece of shit is old enough to be your daddy, and he's going to criticize you? What kind of alternate reality is he living in?"

The young beauty leaned her head back against my chest and pulled my arms tighter around her. God, I could tear his heart out.

"Look," I said, "in the real world that scumbag wouldn't even have the right to talk to you, much less criticize you. Think about it. If that guy saw you at the mall he wouldn't even have the balls to look you in the eye. He would be too intimidated to even talk to you, and if he did, you wouldn't even give him the time of day, literally."

She turned back around to face me and raised her eyebrows in thought, but she didn't smile. "That's true," she agreed.

"If that fat-assed piece of shit had the balls to ask

you what time it was, you would like, 'Get away from me you squid.'" That got a smile out of her.

"I'm not like that," she said.

"I know, sweetie, but you know what I mean. This guy comes in here pissed off at the world and takes it out on you. He thinks because he spent twenty bucks to get in here and ten bucks per round that it gives him the right to be an asshole."

"I didn't do anything to him. All I did was ask him if he wanted a dance, and he was like, 'You should get implants and maybe join a gym.' Fucking jerk."

I made a mental note to deliver one more well deserved beating before the end of the night.

"I know, baby, but look at it this way: His boss treats him like the piece of shit he is, all day at work. He gets home and his wife is screaming at him because his kids are assholes. He can't talk to his friends about it because they'll just call him a pussy. So he comes in here and takes it out on you. It doesn't make it right, but hey, that's why we get the big bucks, right?"

"I guess. Maybe if he takes it out on me, his wife and kids won't have to listen to him bitch," she said hopefully.

"Exactly." I said, but I didn't believe it. I knew that if he was an asshole to a strikingly beautiful naked young woman, he wasn't going to be any better to his wife. "See, you're saving some woman a lot of heartache." She didn't buy it any more than I did, but she reached up and pecked me on the cheek for the effort. I patted that amazing behind. "Now get back to work and don't let him ruin your night."

"Thanks," she said as she wandered back into the crowd, her wound freshly bandaged over for the next prick to tear at.

****

Sometimes it is painfully obvious who is the stronger of the sexes. As a man, if a woman rejected us by telling us we had a lousy body and our penis was too small, we would never recover. If we didn't instantly blow our brains out, we would crawl under a mound of self-doubt and pity, curl up in a fetal ball, and curse the gods who had cursed us. There is not a man on Earth who could take that type of abuse night after night in the course of his work. Yet exotic entertainers take it, survive it and deal with it as part of the job.

What sort of woman becomes an exotic entertainer? Those who can.

If being an exotic entertainer was easy, every woman would do it. Why not? There is the money, the power, the freedom; you come and go as you please. No set hours. No set days. Being an exotic entertainer is not all about beauty or youth or an altered sense of morals. It is about being psychologically strong enough to survive what men can dish out. There is no *type* of woman who chooses to become an exotic entertainer, no more than there is a type who becomes a deli owner, lawyer, accountant or school teacher. Women from every background and upbringing work in this business with possibly only one core trait in common: the strength to survive.

Some of the most successful exotic entertainers I have met, have been married with loving families. Their drive was not so much the money and lifestyle that exotic entertaining afforded, but the attention and the power it yields.

Is an exotic entertainer powerful? More so than you can probably imagine. Much more so than simply being the ultimate feminist.

The following is a paraphrased (altered) Aesop fable:

The Sun and the Wind are having an argument over who is stronger, when they witness a man walking down the street on a chilly winter day. The man is wrapped against the cold in a long overcoat.

The Wind, claiming he is the stronger of the two, bets the Sun that he can tear the man's coat from him, leaving him with nothing to protect him against the elements.

The Sun agrees to the contest.

The Wind begins by whipping up a gale of icy blasts. The man, so assaulted, grips his coat tighter around himself and trudges on. The Wind becomes infuriated and blows harder and harder until the man can no longer make headway, but only grips his coat with all his might and leans against the Wind. Finally exhausted, the Wind subsides, and it is the Sun's turn.

The Sun glows brightly, warming the day so much that the man, finding no more use for his coat, strips it from himself and basks in the glow of the Sun.

A successful exotic entertainer gains her power in much the same way: A powerful man, an executive in his own company, may control, with an iron fist, all that surrounds him, until an attractive woman with a kind word and a smile, makes the tyrant as giddy as a schoolboy with his first crush. I have seen it thousands of times, applied in the real world (the real world of strip clubs, in any case), and *that* is power. For those scoffing at my example and definition of power, you are more than welcome to try it yourself and see where it gets you.

Even I, who could easily beat the executive to a bloody and sobbing pulp, could not pry a car, apartment and thousands of dollars from this man, and keep him coming back for more. All my power is trivialized compared with that of an intelligent exotic entertainer.

Intelligent exotic entertainer? Oxymoron? Believe that if you wish. The stereotype of the stupid stripper actually makes the job of an entertainer that much easier.

It is as intelligent to believe all entertainers are of low intelligence as it is to believe all politicians are womanizing, dope-smoking perjurers who do not believe oral sex counts as sex, or all doctors are frauds, all accountants are thieves, all lawyers are amoral, and all priests are pedophiles.

What common perceptions have classified as stupid is often simply a case of youth and inexperience. How smart were you at nineteen? How smart would you have been at nineteen with five hundred dollars a day in your pocket? Personally, I doubt I would have made it to twenty.

How many readers of this book are published authors? I know more than one exotic entertainer who is.

One exotic entertainer I know is a young woman whom I watched go from stripper, to cocktail waitress, to bartender, to lawyer, all in a span of about six years. She was recently elected to a municipal judgeship—the first female judge in Henderson, Nevada. Working at the strip club put her through law school.

Actresses, professional ice skaters, professional Las Vegas and Broadway show dancers, models, sandwich shop owners, health club professionals, massage technicians, marketing directors, hotel administrators, school teachers, singers, wives and mothers.... I make use of these examples to appease those who measure intelligence and worth by vocation. It is a narrow and somewhat ignorant measure that confuses education with intelligence, but if that is the measure you prefer, the examples can be presented endlessly.

What do you really think happens with the millions of exotic entertainers who retire from the business each year? Do they all simply drop off the face of the earth, or are they shipped off to the great stripper trailer park in the sky? Your bank teller, your clothing accessory designer, your HOA president, your dog trainer, your day care provider...all these and more are what become of former exotic entertainers. It is typically a small, brief chapter in a life, and then life goes on.

So who are these exotic entertainers, where do they come from, where are they headed, what makes them do what they do? It would be arrogant and presumptuous of me to assume, after only twenty years of witnessing, observing and interacting with these women, that I have a clue about the female psyche. No one knows who a woman is or why she does what she does. (Existential?) Women are still a complete mystery to me. A wonderful, exciting, awe-inspiring mystery even to themselves, I sometimes think. I can give examples, though, and if you can open your mind, your conclusions may be as valid as mine.

Susan: a beautiful woman with a presence that inspired wonder in the most jaded. Previously married to a man with an infidelity problem, Susan entertained, I believe, because it was what she was born for. Like an elite athlete—a sprinter who has the genetics and psychological makeup to be the fastest in the world—Susan was born to make others happy in all ways. Mesmerizing to the point of legend, kind, caring, happy with life and what it offered. The most positive, joyous, life-affirming individual I have ever met. (Now CFO for Satsu Multimedia Corp.)

Deanna, the power monger. Deanna entertained because it put her in a position of control over the most powerful individuals in the world. Policy makers and leaders of every sort fell to their knees before Deanna. Deanna's mantra seemed to be; why be a judge, president or king when your word can be obeyed by them all? Loving mother and wife, Deanna chooses to wield her power in other ways now (only for good, of course).

Jessica; willful, determined, indomitable. Not even cancer can subdue this spirit. Jessica couldn't dance a lick when I met her. Not a step. No rhythm, no natural ability, just an idea and a pervasive will. She used every penny of the little money she earned as a reluctant entertainer to learn to dance at the best dance studios in Las Vegas. She used the Cheetahs stage to train and practice and hone her craft. The patrons criticized her for trying to be a real dancer. The students and instructors of the dance studios criticized for being a stripper. Jessica never quit. She is now a highly sought after show dancer, ice skater, and choreographer who will one day (never doubt this) own an elite dance studio of her own. Her students will be fortunate to have an instructor who will not sit in judgement of their dreams, or methods of achieving them.

I have known thousands of exotic entertainers and I could go on with thousands of examples, each unique, each a valid person with valid dreams and goals. Who are they? They are us, no better, no worse, simply stronger in some respects, and much more delicate in others.

"But I know a lot of strippers, and they get drunk every night, use drugs, are promiscuous," some will squawk. It seems everyone knows someone who is willing to make that claim. As if they really knew. It is too easy to pile these attributes on exotic entertainers.

Consider that bar employees drink more than the norm, not necessarily entertainers, but bar employees. Statistics hounds out there should love this: a profession with a higher incidence of alcoholism (and suicide) than strippers: police officers.

The youth of our nation use drugs, not necessarily strippers, but people between the ages of fifteen and twenty-five. Many exotic entertainers do happen to fall into this demographic, but if you are looking for a high incidence of drug dependency, you need look no further than your local university.

Strippers are sluts? Get over it. Sexually promiscuous behavior is beginning well before high school—individuals far too young to even have considered exotic entertaining as a vocation. Ask any twenty-three-year-old club kid and he will tell you. It is much easier to get laid in a dance club than a strip bar. Funny how a woman can be declared a slut for *not* sleeping with someone.

Recently, I read in the paper that comedian Chris Rock, in a show at the MGM Grand, said that his only job in life was to keep his daughter "off the pole," and "they don't grade fathers, but if your daughter is a stripper, you [messed] up."

"They" do grade fathers, Chris (we all do), and if preventing your daughter from being an exotic entertainer is what you consider to be your only job, you have already failed miserably. I realize Chris Rock is a comedian, and his comments were intended to be funny, but if having your daughter perform as an exotic entertainer is the absolute worst fate you can imagine, you have no business being a father at all. I am positive the majority of people can name more comedians/actors who have destroyed their lives, and the lives of their families, with drugs, alcohol and ignorant and self-destructive behavior, than they can name strippers who have done the same. The comedy profession is a very strange one to be pointing fingers in this respect. However, if this is Mr. Rock's only concern, and his daughter shares any of his physical traits, I am sure he is safe from the fate which he dreads.

Regardless of the context, the statement (and the fact that it was included by the reporter in his story) illustrates how pervasive the negative stereotypes and prejudices are.

Just a note: How many cases of strip club employees molesting children have you ever heard? How many cases of clergy molesting children have you heard? Who do our children really need protection from?

If you persist in your prejudice and unenlightened beliefs, I will not begrudge you your ignorance. I have several naive opinions myself, and have a tendency to inflict them upon others at every opportunity (annoying, isn't it?). I will, however, offer the following space to one who would know even better than I of this subject.

The following essay was a gift. It was donated to me for this book by a favorite entertainer. I received it with the request that if I ever wrote this book, it would be included. I proudly include it in the hopes that even if you do not find my own observations compelling, hers might help you see in a more informed light.

## THE POWER OF PREJUDICE
### GENEROUSLY CONTRIBUTED BY J.

Stupid, drug-addicted slut, that's me. At least that is your perception of me. In polite company you might generously use the more endearing term, stripper.

I am not a stripper, although in common parlance, that is the generic term for a twenty-two-year-old woman who entertains men in a nightclub, wearing nothing more than a flimsy g-string and teetering on a pair of ridiculously high heels. "Stripper" evokes romantic images of those marvelous performers of yesteryear. Elegant women strutting proudly in the center of a spotlighted stage. Flesh and blood goddesses dressed in their marvelous costumes of sequins and feathers. A bass drum and cymbal keeping time for an elaborately choreographed routine that transformed the simple act of disrobing into a work of pure erotic art. That is not what I do. My art lies less in the erotic shedding of garments and more in the exploitation of a man's weaknesses.

When you call me stupid, I know you don't mean it. Stupid pertains to lacking normal intelligence or understanding. I know this is not what you mean. You have not taken the time to know me well enough to know what I understand and what I do not. I believe what you probably mean by stupid, is ignorant. Or if you are feeling especially benevolent, young, uneducated, naive, possibly even innocent. I will readily attest that I am ignorant of many things, but we are all ignorant of some matters, aren't we? I do not take offense at your calling me ignorant. I am ignorant: as to how a bill is signed into law, or how to rebuild a carburetor. I am even ignorant as to how all those ones and zeroes translate into the images I see on my computer screen. Fortunately, for all of us, ignorance is a condition that can be remedied. I am becoming educated on how a bill becomes law, and I have a book that seems fairly comprehensive on how to rebuild a carburetor. (I believe I will choose to remain ignorant on how computer binary code works. There are some things better left unknown.)

In many other areas, I am extremely well-educated. For example, I can explain to you, in definitive terms, the rules for using periods and commas with quotations. I can teach you how to itemize deductions for a business loss on your tax forms. I could even tell you precisely why that kindly sixty-year-old business owner chooses to spend an hour each week pouring out his heart to a seemingly vacuous young woman like myself. Ignorant? Possibly. Stupid? I like to think not.

You furrow your brow, and shake your head sadly,

and confide to your assenting friends that all strippers are addicted to drugs. "It's sad, really," you simper. So tragic. Drug addicted? To this I readily confess. It is nearly physically hurtful to me to imagine making it through a full day without a cup of Starbucks coffee or the half-dozen aspirin that keep my high-heel-tortured feet from qualifying me for a handicapped license plate. Caffeine and aspirin: my drugs of choice. Yes, I do know many topless entertainers who use illicit drugs. Tragically, I also knew many high school students who used the same drugs. Even the former, and current, U.S. Presidents claim to have used more illicit drugs than I. The image of the drug-addicted stripper, perpetuated by Hollywood and urban legend, in my experience is greatly exaggerated. Of the thousands of exotic entertainers I have known, the incidence of true drug addiction is rare. It saddens and bewilders me to hear you speak of this matter with which you are, at best, only vaguely familiar. Try to imagine a junky looking for her next fix and attempting to maintain the composure and wherewithal necessary to derive an income from cynical, suspicious men twice her age.

So why do you, even now, persist in your belief? Why do you stare at me with condemnation in your eyes? You who have never seen the inside of a strip club, nor had the opportunity to walk a single step in my (eight-inch platform) shoes.

You watch me perform, my bare skin tinted red by the colored lights. You watch me writhe like a wanton harlot. Close enough to be abraded by the coarseness of his clothes. Close enough to see a bit of something wilted and green wedged between his teeth. Close enough to smell the fresh alcohol over the rancid bile of his persistent ulcer, and you know I am a woman of loose character. Your assumption is one that causes me to shudder with tears, but not for the reasons you might imagine. After all, I can no longer tolerate the touch of a man. Any man. A man's touch has come to represent labor and degradation, and a sad, sick, feeling of desperation and despair. Every sort of hateful, spiteful, rude, venomous remark, I have endured. Vile anger, vomited from the crude, the resentful, the desperate and desolate, has been heaped upon me until I have choked on it. I have come away with, not hate, but worse, a numb disinterest. No feeling at all. I have faith that one day the feeling of non-feeling will pass and I once again will be able to look upon a man, touch a man, and not be numbed.

Your belief that I take pleasure from the requirements of my craft is to believe a waitress serves your food because she is irresistibly drawn to a life of servitude. What I do is a job. I am a performer, and I perform well. You, of course, may feel free to call me a slut—a hateful word used to belittle and hurt—and I will forgive you your ignorance. I may even manage a smile at the irony.

To you I am a stupid, drug-addicted slut. You are repulsed by me, confused, intimidated. You fear me. You may belittle, berate and degrade me if you wish. You may even find it in your heart to hate me, and I will pity you and pray for you.

Your prejudice is my power, your pride my weapon, your ignorance my tool. Think nothing good of me, and my good will overwhelm you. If your pride can release your prejudice, you may find me—just a woman.

\*\*\*\*

## So, What Now?

You're a twenty-six-year-old woman with a high school diploma. You live in a two-thousand dollar per month apartment, drive a new BMW with six-hundred dollar per month payments, and matching quarterly insurance costs. Your closet is filled with designer clothes, your apartment with top of the line furniture, your ears, fingers, belly button, nose, nipples and god knows what else, is covered and filled and dangling, with diamond, gold, and platinum jewelry. You have been making several hundred dollars cash per night, working whenever you feel like it, over the past two years, and now it is all about to end.

I have just described an upper level Las Vegas topless entertainer. She has worked her way up to her standard of living through persistence, intelligence and diligence.

Making a living as a topless entertainer is exceedingly difficult. Most entertainers never make it to the top of their craft, and most women, regardless of education, IQ level, or desire, could never manage it for any price. The job wears on a woman emotionally and physically, and can absolutely crush all but the strongest and most self reliant.

No one can perform this job forever. On occasion you will see those who try. Those enticing forty-year-old women, frighteningly well preserved, competing with girls young enough to be their daughters (and many times continuing to excel). But eventually—and much sooner for the vast majority of women—they must give up the vocation, and get on with their lives.

What can a woman, accustomed to living extremely well, coming and going at her job as she pleases, affording every bauble she sees and desires, driving a dream car, living in a dream apartment...do after she can no longer perform the job of an exotic entertainer?

It is important to note that most topless entertainers do not retire from the business due to physical reasons. It is not an inability to maintain the physical form found desirable in strip clubs that drives women from the business. It is the mental aspect that by far claims the majority of topless entertainers; day after day of enduring ignorant remarks and ignorant stereotypes from an ignorant society; scorning, and berating, and disrespecting a person for their choice of livelihood. A hardened mature individual would eventually break under the strain. A young woman, still developing her sense of self, can be devastated.

Eventually, the wealth, and freedom, and power that comes with being a successful entertainer can no longer mute the trials, and it is time to quit.

So what then? It may not be something most people consider, but performing as a topless entertainer is simply brief episode in a woman's life, a few years of enduring the emotional stress, and then she goes on to do something else. But what? How do you bring yourself to punch a clock for an hourly wage after earning six figures a year on your own time, being your own boss? It is possibly the toughest hurdle one can face, and nearly every entertainer must face it eventually, often without conscious preparation for what's next.

This is not to say that I have not known topless entertainers who used their generous income to set up their future—poured every dime into what would result in living their dream—but as with nearly every twenty-something individual, in any walk of life, those individuals are few and far between. I would not be so presumptuous to suggest that all topless entertainers reading this save their money or buy real-estate or invest in stocks or use their earnings to prepare for their future (it took me twenty years as a topless bar bouncer to find my own way. I doubt mine is the best road, or advice to follow), but I will declare this self evident statement: It does end.

On that day, that day you can not bring yourself to endure the ignorant remarks and comments and assumptions any longer, and you decide to leave this chapter of your life behind, know another extremely difficult task lies ahead. Also know you are far more prepared than your contemporaries. You are far more prepared than even you might imagine.

You have skills and talent and traits that, although they can not be put on a resume, will serve you nonetheless: You know people—their strengths and weaknesses, their fears and dreams. You can not be misled: You have already heard all the lies and false promises. You can not be offended: You have survived the worst and the best men have to offer. You have the mental toughness and fortitude to excel at anything you choose to do.

So when that day comes, and you ask yourself, what do I do now? The answer is, absolutely anything your heart desires.

*"I hate to advocate drugs, alcohol, violence, or insanity to anyone, but they've always worked for me."*
*- Hunter S. Thompson*

# DRUGS

"**B**ut the president smoked it," she said, responding to my look of disgust.

"Ex-president," I corrected. "And he also used cigars on chubby interns young enough to be his daughter, lies, cheats, steals.... I don't think he is your best example. How about our current president? He only gets drunk and does coke." The sarcastic irony was lost on her.

"Eeeww, coke," she wrinkled her button nose at the thought. "I won't touch that shit. It makes me stupid. I just like smoking a little of the chronic, you know, the natural stuff."

"Heroin is natural too, it comes from poppies," I countered.

Yea, but they process it and stuff. I just like my weed. It keeps me mellow. You trying to tell me you never smoke weed?"

"God no," I said, laughing. "I wasn't born with enough brain cells to go around killing them off indiscriminately."

"You don't do any drugs?" She asked.

"I love coffee. But I also indulge in way too much chocolate, eat far too much sushi and have an undeniable addiction to beautiful, naked twenty-year-old girls." As usual, my attempt at humor came off as pompous, arrogant, condescending and sexist.

"At least I don't do crank or ecstasy or G or any of that stuff," she said.

Now I had made her defensive. I tried to atone, better I had tried to stay quiet. "I used to drink a lot, before I got in the bar business and saw how stupid drunks were."

She happily latched on to my last. "Yea, and I'm not drunk every night like some of these people."

"That's true," I conceded.

"I don't even like to drink that much, it makes me sick," she said. I nodded and grunted in agreement. "Besides, it's fattening. I could be doing a lot worse."

"That is also true," I agreed wholeheartedly, and in fact she was right. I have seen it much worse.

****

Far be it from me to posture on the ethical or moral uses of politically illicit drugs. I am nobody's daddy, and I have plenty of faults of my own I need to address before I begin on the world's ills. On this subject I am simply an observer and relater of what I have seen.

The drugs of choice in a topless lounge vary from location to location, I am sure. I am also sure that drugs in topless lounges mirror drugs in contemporary society, so much so that it varies from generation to generation depending on what was being used when they were in high school.

When I worked in the popular clubs of San Diego, California, in the mid to late 1980s, crystal meth (methamphetamine) was by far the drug of choice. It was easier to count the entertainers who were *not* wired than to try and add together all the ones who were. Even to this day, twelve years later in another state, I can spot a girl from Southern California by her twitchy, spastic demeanor and sallow and drawn complexion. God, I hate that drug. Meth has, in my estimation, destroyed more beautiful young Southern California girls than all other drugs combined. These days I am greatly spared the effects of the drug except for the occasional entertainer from the People's Republic of California, and, of course, that sad, pathetic, seemingly wired-to-the-gills Cheetahs shift manager. (Just recently this manager was moved to the new club, sparing everyone at Cheetahs the nearly comically incoherent, quivering, sweating lump of...).

How could a night shift manager of a successful Las Vegas topless lounge function wired out of his mind on methamphetamine? Not very well. I'm not sure what else it could possibly be that causes this crazed individual to sweat uncontrollably for eight hours straight (possibly more, I don't know him outside work) if not for meth. To watch the poor fellow race around the club aimlessly, blurting out incomprehensible partial thoughts that sound more like the coughing and sputtering of a poorly tuned race car, than a human language, would be comical if it weren't so pathetic. It appears to me that, in an attempt to cover his addiction, which would manifest itself in dramatic weight loss, he may counterbalance his meth use with massive amounts of anabolic steroids. The steroids would keep the weight on, the meth would keep him flying—treading water, becoming neither phenomenally muscular nor emaciated. The combination would seem maintainable except for the catastrophic psychological effects it inflicts. Methamphetamine prevents the holding of a coherent thought. Anabolics promote hyper-violent and aggressive behavior: a very bad combination.

Many have felt the irrational, psychotic wrath of this manager and his bizarre drug cocktail. I believe one patron's life may have ended as a result.

For those who imagine I am only supposing, and have no real basis of fact to support my observation, know this; When a police officer pulls over a drunk driver and determines he is under the influence, the officer is fairly certain he is correct even before the test results come back confirming his suspicions. Now, know that I have tens of thousands times more experience with meth and anabolics than the typical patrolman has with DUI. I have seen it, every day, many times a day, for nearly twenty years. Yes, I am confident in my assessment.

Behind marijuana, anabolic steroids may be the most common drugs abused in a topless lounge. I can think of only two, out of twelve, bouncers I work with at Cheetahs Las Vegas who are not on permanent cycles of steroids. Management likes its bouncers big. Not because of their increased ability to handle themselves in a physical confrontation, but because there are fewer customers willing to engage in physical confrontations with a two-hundred-eighty pound steroid-enhanced behemoth.

To claim a particular Cheetahs Las Vegas manager is a steroid dealer would be unfair—there seems to be no drug he cannot provide you with. If it is made, he can get it, and he is more than happy to sell it to you. From legitimate prescription drugs to the street bathtub variety, all you have to do is ask.

Drug dealers beware; if you get caught selling drugs in Cheetahs, you will catch a beating. Not only does the drug dealing manager hate competition, he samples his own wares. He is a holy terror when you get him going—like a bull dog on crack—and nothing gets him going faster than cutting in on his business.

The one exception to the "no dealers" rule, is a particular doctor, with some rather interesting fetishes, who will write you a prescription for anything an ailment has been invented for. Just mention your preference, and he'll phone it in for you. Drug dealing through your local pharmacy. As long as "Doc" is provided with the opportunity to fuel his deviance, the Cheetahs drugstore will never run dry.

I have found that the Cheetahs management team seem to prefer painkillers; a symbolic choice considering their suffering at the hands of the club owner. Loritabs might as well be M&Ms at the rate they are devoured, though any depressant or pain killer from Valium to Ketamine apparently will do in a pinch. God forbid you mention to Cheetahs management that you have a headache. You will be offered a pharmacy full of choices in volume sufficient to numb a harpooned whale.

Strangely enough, the disc jockeys I have known are often throwbacks to the '80s, not only in their preferred music selection, but in their drug of choice. You would think you were watching an Oliver Stone movie when you witness a DJ shove eight lines of cocaine up his nose in as many hours. Again, none of my business, but lord, there's another moronic drug in my opinion.

How stupid do you have to be to live your life for cocaine? Here is what I mean. I'll spare the DJ's name, because stupidity and addiction are rather innocuous crimes in most cases. I watched this grown man, father and husband, put so much cocaine up his nose that even taking home twelve to fifteen hundred dollars per day, five days per week, this individual ended up having to room with a manager, and bum rides to work, because he couldn't afford a home or car, or ultimately, his family. It boggles my mind.

I have noticed the younger customers, the twentysomethings, of late have gravitated to the fashionable drugs circulating the rave and dance clubs. Ecstasy and GHB are nearly required fare for kids heading out for a night of club-hopping. Alcohol seems passe to these customers when they are flying high on designer drugs. Bottles of water and energy drinks are consumed by the gallon, enabling most clubs to charge exorbitant rates for such benign libations. If you watch a club kid closely, you might notice he is carrying two bottles of water, one for his GHB, and one with simply water to keep him hydrated from the ecstasy. An even closer look might reveal two cell phones clipped to his belt. One cell phone is for making constant phone calls (apparently you need lots of stimulation when you are on "X"). The other cell phone is for carrying his drugs. The battery of the phone will be hollowed out for a inconspicuous drug cash (inconspicuous except, who needs two cell phones in a night club?).

More mature customers still seem to rely on the old standby, alcohol, for their mind-altering experiences.

My fear is for the next generation, the children who are now in elementary school and are being started on speed to manage their Attention Deficit Disorder. Again, I'm not a father, but isn't it just possible that a nine-year-old child is simply active in his imagination, and bored easily? Could it be natural for kids to lack desire to sit still in a boring classroom for hours on end? Does he have to have a disorder? Do all those children really need to be drugged? Just a thought from someone who has been listening to people rationalize their drug habits for twenty years. It's bad enough when an adult decides to abuse their own minds and bodies, but parents willingly doing it to their own children.... End of rant.

## AN IRONIC NOTE:

Over this past year I had the opportunity to work for—what many consider—the premier after-hours dance club here in Las Vegas. Very top end, very classy, very expensive (very French).

In my first month at this after-hours club, I witnessed more drug use and deviant behavior than in my twenty years of strip club security work combined.

This experience left me with the shocking knowledge that I had been living a sheltered life (as a strip club bouncer!).

## Speaking of drugs Dealers, did I work for the FBI?

That may sound like a stupid question on the surface, but in the wake of Operation G-sting, I have to wonder.

The FBI implanted an undercover snitch into Cheetahs to gain information on Mike Galardi and his relationship with politicians in San Diego and Las Vegas. Tony Montagna (no, I'm not kidding. That's the name he chose), slimed his way into a position as Head of Security for Cheetahs in both cities by providing Mike Galardi with a supposedly dirty cop who could give him inside information on upcoming vice raids and such.

Tony Montagna was a drug dealer. This was apparently no secret to the FBI. As a matter of fact, that was how they got their hooks on him in the first place. Apparently he had been caught dealing steroids, and to avoid prosecution, he had turned into a snitch for the Feds.

While Tony Montagna was Cheetahs Head of Security, he and the FBI built a case against Galardi and several politicians for bribery and political corruption. All they had to do to achieve that amazing feat was overlook the civil rights violations, racial profiling, beatings, fraud, drug dealing...that were taking place in the club under their watch.

Tony Montagna, an admitted drug dealer, phony hit man (he claimed he once took $20,000 for a hit he never completed because the client had no one to complain to), and all around upstanding citizen—a man who was being paid by the FBI to spy on Galardi—was my direct supervisor. I guess that means I *did* work for the FBI.

"Big John," a friend and fellow Cheetahs bouncer, told me he bought his steroids, growth hormone, and assorted other black market pharmacuticals from FBI snitch Tony Montagna. Big John can't testify to that now, because Big John is dead—a victim of intensive drug abuse.

I blame Big John for his own death: He shouldn't have been taking the drugs. I blame Tony Montagna for dealing the drugs to Big John. I blame the FBI for turning a known drug dealer loose in Cheetahs. I blame myself for not calling the police and turning Tony Montagna in.

I miss Big John. The girls miss him too. I know his wife misses him. He was a good guy.

*"You have been weighed in the balance*
*and you have been found wanting."*
*- Inscription on Nezzebenezzer's tomb*

## MANAGEMENT

"*S*omeone in this room will not be working for us within the next three weeks. Someone here will force us to fire them by doing something we specifically asked them not to do." The GM (General Manager) always started the meetings with the same ominous announcement. I'd been to all of them, security meetings that is, and I had his schtick down pretty well by now.

Cheetahs has a theory, espoused by the former batting cage manager (who would give the club's owner free time in the cages), now Cheetahs latest head of security: Fire three people every meeting, and it will keep everyone else in line.

Actually, the whole concept of an employee meeting at Cheetahs was a joke. Nothing specific was ever discussed, nothing ever resolved, nothing ever altered or confirmed. It was all threats, vague inferences and general nonsense about doing things right. Management like the way things worked. They liked the eight hundred dollars cash a night they were pocketing. They liked not knowing how it got there.

The GM continued. "This business is about customer service. We have to give the customers a reason to come back. We have to do it better than the other guy. There are a dozen strip clubs in this town already and there are more on the way. We're doing good now, but we want to keep it that way."

Rah, rah, rah, customer service, my ass. It was about herding as many bodies through the doors as possible, regardless of their safety and comfort, using absolutely any means or method possible. Lately, that method had been to bribe the cab drivers with twenty five dollars per customer they brought us—a full five dollars per head more than our competitors. How substantial is five dollars? Realize the cab drivers I've known would sell their mothers to a snuff film for two bits. We were now getting customers who had thought they were getting a ride to Caesar's Palace.

Business in a strip club depends on one thing and one thing only: the girls. If you have the most and best girls, you have the most and best customers. End of story. Now if we could only get management to learn this fact.

Generally, the twelve bouncers crowding the cramped office kept quiet at these meetings. The less you said, the faster you could get out of there. It was a rule that would bring the wrath of the other bouncers if violated.

"We've heard rumors..." Oh God, here it comes, I thought, as the GM spoke through his most serious and concerned facade. "...that some of you have been selling tables for fifty, sixty, a hundred dollars and up. We don't want our customers to have to buy a seat when they come in here. We want everyone to be able to to have a good time. The guy offering five dollars for a seat is just as important as the guy offering a hundred dollars. If Mike hears of anyone taking a hundred dollars to seat someone, over someone who has offered five dollars, that person will no longer be with us."

Sometimes the shit just got too silly, too deep, too thick...and forced my mouth open. "You don't differentiate between a hundred-dollar tipper and a five-dollar tipper?" I asked what should have been a rhetorical question.

"Of course not," the GM scowled. "Why should the guy with a hundred dollars get to sit when the guy with five has to stand?" So much for rhetorical.

"Well, gee, I don't know, maybe because the guy who is willing to spend a hundred dollars just to sit down is likely to spend more money on everything, like drinks and dances. You know, take care of your high-rollers. Millionaires don't like to stand in a crowded room when a bunch of ratty used car dealers got a table in front of them for five bucks...just a thought." I added the last in response to the blank look I was receiving, not only from the GM, but the assistant GM, and the club's lawyer, the other two upper-management types who presided over the meeting.

"Well, Mike doesn't want to see it, so if you get caught, you're out of here, okay?" The GM waited for an answer.

"Sounds great. I'm all over it," I replied. "It's not my club."

That's right," he said, making sure I got it.

It was readily obvious to everyone in the room why I'd worked seven different topless clubs in the past twenty years, and never had the opportunity to quit a single one: I had a hard time keeping my mouth shut.

None of this really mattered anyway. The way it really worked would never change. Nobody was going to bust his balls getting a table for someone holding a five-dollar bill. It was easy to cover. The club was standing-room-only every night. So we couldn't find a table, no big deal. Someone offered a twenty or more, and a table would miraculously clear. Just luck of the draw, I guess. There was always a move a good floorman could make. Some scumbag's not drinking, not tipping, not buying dances, sitting around with his skin a shade too dark. All that combined with the fact that not a single manager in this joint had enough experience on the floor to know the difference between a "good" move and a bribe move. Hell, I could probably move the GM himself off a table and he would think it was a legitimate move.

A young, idealistic (spelled foolish), ultimately unfortunate floorman had once actually tried to do it their way: A party of customers had offered the goofy little sap forty dollars to procure them a table. Typical transaction. No big deal, or shouldn't have been. The floorman had several (lower-paying) requests for seating already and told the forty-dollar party it would have to wait until he got his other parties seated. The forty-dollar party complained to management that it had offered the floorman forty dollars to find a table, and the bouncer had refused. The floorman was immediately sent home (not fired, that announcement would come later on his answering machine), accused of attempting to jack up the price of a table from forty dollars to something more—the assumption management instantly made. Had the floorman simply taken the forty dollars and sat the customers, not only would he have been forty dollars richer, the club would have been entertaining a valued group of customers, and he still would have been employed. As it happened, the club lost the customers, and the floorman lost his job. So much for the club's way of doing things.

Part of the problem with Cheetahs managers is they did not work their way up through the club. None of them, not one, had ever held another position in the establishment where they might learn how things worked. Each of the upper managers had either come from a long-term relationship with the owner (high school buddies) or had access to perks for the owner. (For example: one former head of security, a favorite perk management position, also worked for a professional sports team and could get the Cheetahs owner and his friends onto the sidelines for games. He also claimed to have intimate inside information on who was up for games and who was not; useful information for anyone who likes to bet on sports.)

The manager/bouncer meeting continued: "There also may, or may not be, a problem with whoever is on the back VIP room taking money to let couples pass the line. If that's true, and I'm not saying it is, it's got to stop." The GM eyed each of us in turn to emphasize his point.

It was becoming painfully obvious what the theme of the meeting was really about. The bouncers were making a little money—more than their fifty-dollar shift pay—on the side, and that was unacceptable. Receiving tips in a tipping environment, who woulda thunk it?

My mouth was giving me serious problems today,

as usual. "Of course it's true," I said. "Isn't that the definition of a VIP room, a place for high-rollers to hang out? How do you differentiate the high-rollers from the regular jackoffs if you don't allow the high-rollers to assert themselves?" I asked yet another seemingly rhetorical question. The blank stares I was getting from management told me "rhetorical" was not in their vocabulary.

"Do you have a problem with the way this club runs, Mr. Jordan?"

Oops, I had forced him to break out the "Mr. Jordan." It meant I was on the verge of being sent home myself. "Not at all, sir. I'm just curious."

"They're already paying a hundred dollars for four songs, that's enough."

Maybe subconsciously I was looking to get fired. It surely must have appeared that way to everyone else in the room. "But isn't the guy willing to toke a twenty or more to get in the VIP room a little bit quicker, likely to spend more than just a hundred dollars, maybe five or six? I mean, you have to figure the guy's not going to spend more than ten percent to get in the room, so if he tokes forty, it would stand to reason he'll spend at least four hundred inside...good for the girls, good for the club?"

"We don't pay you enough, is that the problem?" The GM asked sarcastically.

I was well up the creek now. If I shut up now, I still might survive this meeting. If I could just shut up now..."Think about it," I began (just shut up). "If you and Mike went to some strip club and you wanted to go to the VIP room and get some dances (shut the hell up), would you stand in line for twenty minutes waiting, or would you just slip the doorman a toke and move to the front of the line? (Please shut up.) Mike's a millionaire. Millionaires don't wait in line at strip clubs." If I could just shut my mouth.

The GM thought on that a minute—no doubt reflecting on the last time he and Mike had done just that—before he gave the reply I already knew was coming. "What Mike does and what everyone else does are two different things. If you get caught passing the line in the VIP room, you will be sent home."

That ended the discussion, as far as they knew.

Treat high-rollers like common people. It was a concept that was foreign to not only any real topless club employee, but to Las Vegas as a whole. Imagine if the hotel-casinos took that stance. No more comps, no more suites, no more perks of any kind no matter what you had to spend. The hotel-casinos would be headed the same way Cheetahs was—toward the crapper.

"Now let's talk about the dress code." Once the GM had successfully addressed the problem of the bouncers making extra money, it was time to violate a few civil rights. "I am still seeing way too many brothers walking around here, especially after two or three in the morning. I come in here sometimes and it looks like the Moolie-on Rouge. I want you to start enforcing the dress code a little more strictly."

Dress code, right. Since when is the color of your skin considered dress?

I had started a bad precedent. One of the other bouncers spoke up. "Sometimes they go home and change. What are we supposed to do?"

Yet another made his voice heard. "I had this problem the other night when these like, six fuckin' white kids walked out dressed exactly like the brothers at the front door, who I just told couldn't come in because their pants were too baggy."

"Fuckin' white kids wearing that FUBU shit. Don't they know what that means?" Another chimed in.

"Farmers Used to Buy Us," another retorted. The meeting was degenerating quickly.

"Just keep them out. I don't care how you do it. Mike doesn't want to see any more niggers in here. If they fit the dress code, find something else. Their I.D. doesn't look like them...anything." The GM reasserted the original theme of the discussion.

"How could their I.D. not look like them? They all look alike." The club's lawyer made himself heard for the first time. The bouncers snickered politely at the comment.

The GM introduced the club's attorney. "Everybody knows Mike's lawyer? He's here to add a few things the DA wants us to keep in mind. Go ahead." He gave the floor to the attorney.

"First thing is lap dances," the attorney began. "You guys have got to watch for grinding. The girls can't be jerking the guys off with their crotch." Just two weeks earlier I had my ass reamed for suggesting a girl get off the speaker's lap. "So after they grind a little bit, tell them to get off and do something else."

"How long is a little bit?" One bouncer wanted to know.

"A few times," the attorney answered.

"Like three or four?"

"Just don't let the girls grind too much, okay?" The GM was testy with the continual questions.

The attorney resumed. "Another thing is the girls giving out their phone numbers to the customers. We can't have that. Just tell the girls to give the guys fake numbers."

There it was, irrefutable proof: The attorney was a moron. I think every eye in the room widened with disbelief at the suggestion. As far as we knew, a girl couldn't legally give a customer any number, fake or otherwise. It was considered soliciting prostitution. As far as we bouncers had been told, by the vice officers responsible for such matters, it was illegal to even give a girl a pen to write her number with. It was obvious this attorney was not even in the same rule book with the rest of us, much less on the same page, and he was the one giving legal advice? Furthermore, regardless if the vice cops were telling the truth about the legality of giving out phone numbers or not (I suspect not, the cops I have known made up their own rules as they went along) was besides the point. If a cop wanted to arrest a girl for soliciting prostitution based on her giving out a phone number, he would. The arrest was still an arrest, regardless of the outcome in court. An arrest for soliciting prostitution still counted against the club's license, again, regardless of the outcome. A competent lawyer would know this.

At that point I gave up on getting a productive answer out of the meeting. Get back to the original plan, I thought. Keep your mouth shut and you would be out of there sooner.

\*\*\*\*

Western High School, class of 1980, otherwise known as the Cheetahs Management Team. It seems every has-been, wannabe, never-been derelict who knew Mike Galardi more than six months in his youth, has at one point or another, been employed by the lucrative topless club. Not one of them had ever worked in any capacity in any nightclub before. Their total sum of qualifications for obtaining the quarter-million dollar title of Cheetahs Management, was simply they had the overwhelming lack of character that prompted them to strive to become one of Galardi's personal sycophantic groupies.

As I am aware of the folly of using all-encompassing terms such as "everyone", "always", "all", etc., I will offer an exception to the "Cheetahs Management Rule".

A gentleman we will refer to as ND was a good friend. I use the word friend in the context, "A friend is someone who will help you move, a good friend is someone who will help you move the body." ND was head of security for a few years at Cheetahs. I knew him as someone who always had your back. That is, he would always stand up for his crew, even if that meant taking the brunt of a bad situation.

ND had not gone to high school with the owner. He had earned his position through consistent loyalty and hard work. Unfortunately, because of his positive qualities (so rare at Cheetahs) he was charged with transporting the daily receipts to the club's book keeper—in cash.

Why would any business transport eighty thousand dollars cash under the watch of a single employee instead of using an armored car service? Armored car services must sign for every dollar they transport—a written record. You figure it out.

In any case, one day ND was mugged at the foot of the stairs to the downtown book keeper's office, and relieved of the daily receipts. ND survived the mugging (an attack with chemical mace), but was fired upon his release from the hospital. Because ND had lost the money, a single weekend's receipts for the club, he was fired and effectively blackballed from other clubs with the freely spread slanderous rumor that he was a thief. ND took, and passed, a lie detector test. He was never charged with a crime by the police on the case, but Mike Galardi had made his decision, and ND was out.

Why would anyone want to eliminate such a dedicated and fiercely loyal employee and friend? Possibly it was no coincidence that ND's firing coincided with the hiring of the new head of security, a man who also worked for a professional sports team (and provided all the perks that position would make available).

I hope ND feels vindicated knowing that had he remained Cheetahs head of security, the FBI's operation G-sting could have never happened, and Mike Galardi would still own Cheetahs.

Cheetahs management, as a whole, is greatly a parody of Las Vegas lifestyles: One manager, addicted as he is to sports betting, wagered thirty thousand dollars on a single college football game. Even though he was making a quarter-million dollars per year, and claimed to have inside information on the game, this bet would seem extravagant to most. The manager lost that bet, by the way.

With multiple current and former Las Vegas City

Council members (termed managers and advisers) receiving cash pay envelopes weekly, the Cheetahs "office parties" could be a scene straight out of The Sopranos. (A Cheetahs "office party" consists of a high-profile businessman or politician, a willing girl, and a hidden video camera.)

Watching an ethics-challenged councilman approach the back door of the club's office dressed in an over sized coat and baseball cap pulled down over his eyes, as if the disguise might help conceal the features that make the local news nightly, to receive a cash "campaign contribution" would be laughable if not for the fact that Cheetahs concurrently received an okay for another lucrative and coveted topless club location during a following City Council meeting on these matters. (*This passage was obviously written before the FBI's Operation G-Sting that indicted Cheetahs Owner Mike Galardi and several local politicians for offering and accepting bribes—buying votes. The case continues as of this writing.*)

A Cheetahs manager who, in a methamphetamine and steroid-induced rage, beats a customer unconscious and leaves him out back of the club—like so much garbage, to become a target for a passing gang of youths, ultimately ending in the man's death—is nowhere near laughable. The ensuing cover-up that involved death threats on witnesses, and worse, leaving the police impotent in their investigation, is better suited to an Elmore Leonard novel than to real life.

Imagine one middle-aged manager, with the voice and mannerisms of an adult cartoon character (think: Johnny Bravo on steroids), whose sexual exploits are legendary even within the strip club community. Quite possibly the least politically correct person on the planet. This manager is left to run loose in a room full of young topless entertainers, making many popular athletes and celebrity exploits pale in comparison. He represents every imagined and cliche´ statement ever made about the sexual habits of a strip club manager, come to life.

Imagine a manager on the bottom rung, so browbeaten and degraded on a daily basis, that the nearly comatose state he drinks himself into nightly seems a logical and elevated lifestyle choice. (This manager is dead now, reportedly a self-administered DUI victim.) Loni, you are missed.

So your next question nevertheless might be, "Yea, but for a quarter-million bucks per year and all the naked twenty year olds I can shake my stick at, how do I get to become a manager of Cheetahs?"

Like almost everything in life, there is the short route and the long route.

The short route: Grow up with Mike Galardi. Be so generally incompetent that holding a regular job is an impossibility. Let go of all your human pride, and develop yourself into a sycophantic lap dog who quivers and jumps at every ludicrous and asinine whim of the club's owner, or, have something to trade for the privilege, such as an inside track on a professional sports team or a spot on the City Council with an opportunity to make decisions on topless club zoning and related matters.

The long route: Work at the club in some capacity for several years, quietly, unobtrusively, until the owner mistakes your silence, for competence, and places you in a management position (in which case my personal recommendation is to run like hell. Lose the job but keep your soul and your manhood intact).

Bitter? Oh yea, but does it make the facts any less valid or true?

*"I ran the wrong kind of business,*
*but I did it with integrity."*
*- Sydney Biddle Barrows*

*"There's no business like show business."*
*- Irving Berlin*

## BUSINESS AS USUAL

"You still owe us three hundred and twenty dollars!" The Cheetahs bookkeeper's high-pitched, heavily Philippine-accented voice, stung my ear and grated my nerves even over the distance of a phone line.

"But I haven't been working over the past two weeks, remember? I was fired...again." I tried not to laugh at the obviousness of what I felt must be a mistake.

"That don't matter. You still behind from before!" She was shouting now, taking it personally.

"Before when?" I asked. "I'm up to date. I've got a signature next to every payment in my calendar books going back to 1991." I waved my calendar book in the air as I spoke as if to emphasize my point (over the phone?).

I remembered when I had first started the habit of having the manager sign my tax payment book. It was shortly after the first time I was called for being behind on my taxes. That one had cost me nearly two hundred dollars.

Now the Cheetahs bookkeeper was truly angry. "You want me to tell the IRS how much you really make?" She nearly screamed into the phone. I backed the receiver away from my ear and crinkled my brow in mild confusion.

"I certainly hope you are telling them," I said. "I've been paying quarterly taxes for a long time now, so they already know what I make." I had to grin a little. I had been paying extra taxes based on my wages and tips for years, playing it extremely tight and honest. No one in their right mind messes with the IRS, not in a business guaranteed to be audited, eventually. Those IRS guys are just plain mean, even by my standards.

The bookkeeper was silent for a moment (I could nearly hear her grinding her teeth in frustration) before changing her tactics. "Mike won't let you work if I tell him you are behind on your taxes," she said.

Now it was my turn to grind my teeth. She had me. She was right and there were no options. "How much do I owe?" I asked.

"Three hundred and sixty dollars." I could hear the smirk in her voice. A moment ago it had been three hundred and twenty dollars. I guess the extra forty was considered penalty and interest for making her argue with me. I hung up the phone quick before I was out an even four hundred.

I have no idea what had possessed me to even consider arguing with her. The Cheetahs bookkeeper got what she wanted. She always would. If you balanced the few hundred dollars she extorted from you every couple of years against the income of your job with the club, your income always came out ahead. Rumor was, the extortion increased every time the bookkeeper had a new landscaping project for her home, or she was slated for her yearly vacation cruise.

Pay the money or don't work. It was as simple as that.

**** 

At this point, allow me to explain the unique accounting practices of Cheetahs Topless Club (as much as I am able, in any case. I don't truly get it myself). At Cheetahs, employees are paid nightly in cash. I currently receive one hundred dollars for my shift pay. At the end of each week, I am expected to pay back to Cheetahs about twenty dollars per day, or exactly $103.50. The amount stays the same regardless of how many days per week I am working. I am currently working three shifts per week, and the amount has not changed since the days when I was working five.

Still don't get it? Neither do I, but I do have my suspicions. It will no doubt take an army of experienced IRS auditors to sort out Cheetahs books.

There are surely corporate types reading this, calling me an idiot for not pursuing the matter through government channels. And they may be right. Maybe the government regulators would slap the hands of those abusing their leverage and power at Cheetahs, but I would still be out of work. There is no "maybe" to that.

If the IRS had any interest at all in looking into

Cheetahs, it seems to me it would have done so long ago. Twenty-dollar cover charge at the door, five bar cash registers, sixty-five-dollar house fee for entertainers, multiplied times hundreds of entertainers per day. Cash payments to certain city council members, management, employees.... One would think Cheetahs would make an ideal training tape for IRS snoops.

It is not as if the IRS has no effect on Mike Galardi's business dealings. I remember when Mike was buying his first house from a popular developer (with a penchant for office parties). Mike learned that banks report to the IRS any cash transaction over five thousand dollars. He needed in excess of fifty thousand dollars for the down payment for the home. Now understand, I wasn't at the signing of the escrow papers, so I can't say for sure how the down payment was handled, but I do know I was ordered—under the threat of my job—to take $4,995.00 to my bank and purchase a cashier check in that amount on behalf of Mike Galardi. A dozen other Cheetahs employees confided in me that they had been forced to do the same thing. Again, I can't tell you definitively what these cashier checks were used for, but I do know Mike bought the house.

*"It is a truism of American politics that no man who can win an election deserves to."*
*- Trevanian*

*"Politics is supposed to be the second oldest profession. I have come to realize that it bears a very close resemblance to the first."*
*- Ronald Reagan*

## POLITICS

7he first time I met (now former) Las Vegas city councilman, Michael McDonald, was when I accosted him outside the back office door of Cheetahs Topless Club.

I had been patrolling the parking lot outside the club for suspicious individuals, as was my habit when the smoke and noise of the bar got to be too much, when I spotted a man—a portly man—dressed in an oversized parka with a baseball cap pulled down low over his face, lurking outside the side office door to Cheetahs. I watched the man as he stealthily looked over his shoulders and hunched his head down into the collar of his coat, like a villain in a bad fifties detective movie, or maybe like a desert tortoise caught out in the open. I approached the man from behind, looping my way around the parking lot and coming up quietly between the parked cars. You could never be too sure of a man's intentions, standing outside the side door to the office of a strip club at two in the morning, so I figured shouting "hey you" from across the lot might not be my best choice of introduction.

The office held tens of thousands of dollars in its safes, and this wouldn't have been the first time a robbery had been attempted at a strip club where I worked.

When I was within easy reach of the man, I asked, "Can I help you?" You would have thought I had snuck up on him and shouted "boo" at the top of my lungs wearing an Oscar Goodman mask, for the way he reacted.

The man spun to face me, wide eyed and mouth gaping. He stuttered and stammered and looked hurriedly around some more as if to confirm there was no one else looking to give him a heart attack. It was then that I recognized his familiar face, and it was also then that I recognized that we were being robbed, only not in the way I had first imagined.

Michael McDonald had been on the news quite a bit at the time. An ethics charge, or something of the sort, had the city council making headlines, and the chunky, former cop, with the pretty features and ridiculous hairdo, had never been particularly camera shy.

The office door suddenly opened, and Mike Galardi poked his head out and said, "He's okay Brent, he just looks like a scumbag." Mike was smiling his wicked, inside joke smile, that made me believe he had been watching McDonald on the security monitors, standing outside in the cold for quite awhile.

I was told later, through the Cheetahs underground information system (management), that Michael McDonald had come by for his "campaign contribution." Considerate of him to come all the way down here to pick it up in person, I thought.

Over the next few years, Michael McDonald became more and more a regular fixture at Cheetahs—and none to covertly either.

McDonald would roll into Cheetahs with a pair of groupies in tow, and proceed to terrorize every living soul in the club; bouncers, entertainers, and customers alike. "I own this place!" "He works for me (pointing to any employee who happened to be within pointing range), "Jaguars wouldn't even be getting built if it wasn't for me." His greatly exaggerated statements were bellowed at the top of his lungs for anyone, and everyone to hear.

The club would turn into a pathetically comic dance, with bouncers and cocktail waitresses rotating to the opposite side of the club from the tubby tyrant. McDonald would move to one side of the club, we would all move to the other. It was far better to avoid the egotistical little bugger than to give him the opportunity to prove to his friends exactly how much he meant to Galardi.

McDonald was annoying, but his actions never truly seemed that strange to me. It was exactly what I had come to expect from politicians. When the president of the United States was making comments like; "I did not have sexual relations with that woman," and "it depends what the definition of 'is' is," why would you expect more from a city councilman?

Apparently all McDonald's posturing inside Cheetahs were bigger boasts and more liberal fabrications than even I imagined. As far as I know, Michael McDonald has not been charged in the FBI's "Operation G-sting." Maybe it really was a campaign contribution.

\*\*\*\*

## POLITICIANS

Obviously, local politicians have always been a valuable asset to have on any business' payroll. This is not a concept that originated with Cheetahs, or the strip club industry. I suspect that politicians have been accepting bribes as long as there have been politicians and free enterprise. The Las Vegas City Council and Clark County Commission decide on licensing for topless clubs and preside over complaints against the licensing of these establishments. It never hurts to donate a few thousand dollars to a few willing council or commission members to ensure their sympathy to your needs.

Apparently, another even more efficient method of controlling politicians is to outright place them on the payroll as managers or advisers. There were many times I had occasion to see a number of the pay envelopes in the Cheetahs office safe, and they read like roll call at a commission meeting. Some of the more enterprising politicians may even find themselves on the payroll of several competing clubs. Who would expect any more of a politician?

Some might expect more of health departments employees, fire marshals and police, but then again, why? Las Vegas is a tipping town. Why work here if you can't take a tip now and again? Am I suggesting the fire marshal turns his back on Cheetahs when it is double capacity and it takes ten minutes of pushing and shoving to get from the bar to the front door? I would never make that suggestion. Would the police ignore the obvious facts and write up incident reports any way the club tells them simply because they get comped into the club, receive free drinks (on or off duty), and date the occasional cocktail waitress or entertainer? Absolutely not. I would never say such a thing. Would the health department inspector take an unusual bribe to restore an "A" rating? I wouldn't know, but I will relate what I have seen.

A certain female health inspector would raid Cheetahs weekly, nitpicking and searching for violations with an exuberance that would make any anal retentive government employee proud. She would constantly make unveiled, envious reference to the health inspectors who worked the big corporate clients (hotels) who, according to her, would receive gifts such as suite comps and cases of champagne for Christmas and birthdays. Thinking she was openly suggesting a bribe, the club's general manager covertly offered her a C-note. ("Look, you dropped something.") The health inspector was not taking. She continued to tag the club for violations week after week despite the general manager's best efforts. Once the general manager even got the inspector so drunk during one of her inspections, that she climbed on stage and did a couple of turns around the brass pole—not a pretty sight. Still, the harsh inspections continued. What ended the reign of terror? The health inspector one day mentioned that she thought the disc jockey was very attractive. That was all the general manager needed to know. The health inspector and DJ were set up on a date, and the club was spared any further harsh criticisms from the health department. The abuse of that particular DJ at the hands of the general manager was legendary, but that particular event, even in context, had to be some sort of all-time low.

## BLACKMAIL

What happens when it just gets too expensive to bribe everyone who has influence over the club? Blackmail.

Along with a gun and loaded magazine labeled, "For FBI and government use only," the FBI found, in Mike Galardi's desk drawer during the Operation G-Sting raid, a videotape of one city councilman allegedly engaging in an office party at Cheetahs.

An office party consists of a "girl for rent" and a prominent figure given a few moments alone in the Cheetahs office to do whatever two (or more) adults are willing to do.

Now, if you were a city councilman, or other high-profile individual, what would be your first impression if you were invited for a few moments alone in a topless club's office with a beautiful young woman who is determined to cater to your every whim? Would it be, (1) gee, that Mike's such a great guy, getting me laid out of the generosity of his heart, or, (2) that Mike's probably trying to lure me into his office to have sex with this young woman so he can secretly videotape me and use the evidence later to blackmail me into giving him what he wants. If you picked choice number two, you are smarter than not only at least one member of the Las Vegas City Council, but a prominent local home developer as well.

Even if you don't get caught with your pants down (literally), doing business with Cheetahs rarely proves to be profitable as far as I can tell. Even with the obscene amounts of money the club earns, its business practices are appalling. For example, my impression is that it would be difficult to find a carpet-cleaning company in the entire city that has actually been paid for its work at Cheetahs. It seems that as far as the club is concerned, it is easier to stiff the company and find a new one in six months when the carpets are due for their next cleaning. No, I'm not kidding. Many other contractors who are not relied on for repeat service seem to be treated in the same manner.

The light and sound company that installed all those annoying, albeit expensive, lights and that booming sound system so many years ago is still waiting for payment in full. The company that established and maintained two of the Cheetahs websites has been paying for its own expenses for two years now and has never received payment of any kind in any amount. Even the company that shot, produced and distributes the "Girls of Cheetahs" erotic video series has never been paid for its work (even though I personally heard Mike Galardi himself state that it was the nicest production he had ever seen). I could probably go on indefinitely (these examples I have first hand knowledge of) as Cheetahs has been in business for many years, and their business practices don't seem to be changing.

Why so petty? Why, if the club is making millions of dollars per year, can it not fulfill its obligations? Because it doesn't have to, I guess. Possibly Mike Galardi is aware that it would cost a small company, or individual, more to pursue the matter in court than it would to take the loss as a write-off. Other than that, I have no answer.

## COPS

I recently read in the paper that Mike Galardi ratted out the local law enforcement, admitting that he offered them comps and other gratuity for preferential treatment.

The sheriff's response to that claim was that Galardi is a less than reliable source, and he (the sheriff) knows nothing about cops receiving comps at Cheetahs or any other establishment.

I have just one thing to say about that statement: In my opinion, either the sheriff truly doesn't know what his officers are doing, which makes him incompetent to run a major police department, or he is lying. There doesn't seem to be a third option.

Everyone I know who has ever worked in a bar, or restaurant for that matter, knows about the police "gold card." A gold card is a cops badge. It is good for free cover, free drinks, and unfortunately, if he flashes it after he has run up a lap dance tab (and scares the entertainer enough), free lap dances. This is not a secret. Ask any bar employee if he has ever charged a cop a cover, or full price for a drink, or meal, or anything else for that matter. Comping cops is so universal, and such an accepted practice in the establishments I have worked, I find it amusing that the subject is even up for debate. (What's worse, I can't believe I am backing Galardi on this.)

*"After all, he thought he was God."*
*- FBI agent on why it was difficult*
*to negotiate with David Koresh*

## OPERATION G-STING

*A* drug dealing FBI undercover snitch, thousands of hours of secretly taped conversations, the liberal use of a new anti-terrorist law, God knows how many millions of tax dollars...and the Federal Government was able to successfully prove that politicians and strip club owners are not the most honest of people. Congratulations!

The FBI had no doubt conceived Operation G-sting with grandiose dreams of organized crime; money laundering, drugs, prostitution...maybe even something really juicy, like contract killing. And why not? Jack Galardi was, for years, rumored to have been "connected"—his last name ends in a vowel, he owns a chain of strip clubs... His son, Mike Galardi was building his own strip club empire in Las Vegas and San Diego. There had to be something fishy going on.

What did the FBI come up with? No drugs. No prostitution. No money laundering. No contract killing: No organized crime. What they got was a few piss ant local politicians with their hands out. How embarrassing for them. Any twenty-year-old stripper could have told them about those dealings over a lap dance or two.

What a scandal it all was. Operation G-sting made the national news: FBI agents bursting through the doors of a famous Vegas strip club, waving their guns around, herding the entertainers up at gunpoint. As if the entertainers had anything to hide beneath their flossy costumes. As if they had any part in the illicit dealings of the club owner. As if they cared.

If it sounds as if I am making light of the whole mess, I am.

The FBI surely would have known, after only a few days of their undercover sting operation, that there was nothing more going on with Galardi and the local politicians than a simple exchange of cash for favors. Wonderful. Take them down. I'm all for it. Remember, I had to work with those idiots—the politicians and the club owner—every day: There is no love lost. However, as soon as the FBI discovered the truth of the matter, they should have acted. Instead, for over two years, they sat on their behinds and watched the antics continue. They watched the city council and county commission members sell out their cities. They watched their undercover snitch deal dangerous, illegal drugs. They watched civil rights violations, beatings, strong arm robberies, sexual assaults.... They watched it all, and then they brought their charges: Bribery (Galardi offering money), extortion (politicians asking for money), and wire fraud (talking about the whole mess over the phone).

I have been interviewed at length by the news

media about my knowledge of Operation G-sting and the illicit dealings of politicians. I dutifully answered their questions to the best of my ability. As you might have noticed, I have nothing to hide. The whole time I was answering their questions, I was asking myself, "so what?"

Dirty politicians: I haven't met a "clean" one yet.

The papers of every city—around the world—are filled with accounts of politicians doing something illegal, illicit, stupid... Indeed, go back a couple thousand years and read Aristotle: The names have changed. Politics remains the same.

It astounds me that such a fervor has been reached over the revelations of Operation G-sting. If the FBI had never spent those two and a half years, and millions of dollars, breaking up the illicit dealings, what would be the end result? Mike Galardi was paying the politicians to relax lap dance regulations (allow the girls to be closer to the customers) and tighten zoning laws (limit competition from other clubs). Two consenting adults, in a private club, would be allowed a little more contact. Fewer strip clubs would be allowed per block. So what?

Have you ever heard of a strip club employee molesting children? A strip club is not a church. Have you ever heard of strip club employees seducing school kids? A strip club is not a high school. Have you ever heard of strip club employees selling national secrets to foreign countries, outing undercover CIA operatives... The strip club is not the Federal government.

I have outlined the crimes I have witnessed and partaken in, within the eight strip clubs where I worked. They are heinous, but the customers were voluntarily in that environment, and there are many worse crimes.

I suppose my point is, when the government conceived Operation G-sting, it may have had it's priorities slightly askew.

So why the time and expense for this undercover sting operation? It may have been the perfect opportunity for the FBI to try out portions of the Patriot Act on white-collar civilian criminals. Mike Galardi remains the only American civilian to ever have been prosecuted under provisions of the Patriot Act.

By perfect opportunity, I mean, who is going to rush to a strip club owners aid? Who will rush forward and tell the FBI they have overstepped their bounds, when the subject is a strip club owner? It was a great opportunity to "ease" a precedence into being. That thought scares me far more than a corrupt politician.

What Operation G-sting has taught me, is even the FBI sees strip clubs, and their employees, as easy targets: A strip club is the last safe bastion for bigotry and prejudice in this country. Use the term nigger, spick, chink...and you will find yourself in a world of hurt: hate crime violation kind of hurt. Yet it is perfectly acceptable to call someone a stupid stripper, in a hateful, vile, bigoted, prejudiced context. Far too many, including the Federal government, take advantage of this fact.

## AN OPEN LETTER TO LANCE MALONE

*Editor's note: Lance Malone is a former Clark County Commissioner indicted in Operation G-sting for allegedly delivering bribes between Mike Galardi and politicians in both Las Vegas and San Diego. Lance Malone was employed as a lobbyist for Mike Galardi.*

Lance,

You no doubt remember me; I was the Cheetahs bouncer with the shaved head who avoided you at all costs, and rolled his eyes at your inane attempts to impress twenty-year-old strippers with your lies about your importance to the club. What you failed to realize was your pretty features and perfect hair were no match for the BS detector inherent in every successful topless entertainer. I was reminded of your lies then, by your accusations now, in the Operation G-sting trial, against your former employer, Mike Galardi.

Lance, it's time you had a reality check: You were a bag man: Your sole purpose, your entire job description for Cheetahs was to shuttle money from Galardi, to whichever city employee who had their hand out at the time. Basically, that's it.

I am not trying to infer that you did not have an effect on Cheetahs, you did. A horrific effect. Through your inept attempts at "lobbying" (or whatever term you chose that helps you sleep at night), you helped facilitate the downfall of a multimillion dollar topless club empire. You turned a local businessman into a mob boss, and you prompted the FBI to employ the Patriot Act against your employer; the first and only time the all-powerful anti terrorist tool has been used against an American citizen suspected of white collar crime.

This is not to say Mike Galardi is not at least equally responsible for the fate which has befallen him. He is. He, by his own admission, was engaged in illegal activities; bribing public officials.

Mike Galardi made many mistakes, and now he has stepped up to take his licks for those mistakes. But I have to tell you, Lance, I believe Mike's biggest mistake was you. He trusted you, and you led him down a path from which he will never emerge.

Now, you claim you didn't know you were bribing council people with the money Galardi was giving you for that purpose. You dispute his claim that he gave you $10,000 dollars—cash—to pass along to the insatiable politicians with whom you had cultivated your illicit relationships. You seek to discredit your former boss, call him a liar. If I did not find that so pathetically, revoltingly ironic, it would be hysterical.

If you did not deliver that money, then you were not performing the job you were being paid to perform. What other purpose could you have possibly served for Cheetahs Topless Club? You know nothing about the business. You are a former cop and failed politician. As near as I can tell, you were hired for your knowledge of how to accept a bribe, and how to offer one. Other than that, as far as the club was concerned, you were useless.

As it turns out, the fact that you are now under indictment proves that ultimately, *useless* would have been the very best thing you could have been.

Lance, take heart. I do give you one bit of respect and credit: Your cowardice and inability to stand up and take responsibility for your actions seemed to have triggered your self-preservation instinct, and you hired the best criminal defense attorney money can buy. If there is any chance at all of your sliming your way out of your dirty deeds, the legendary Dominic Gentile will show you the way.

However, knowing what I do of you, and having had to listen to Mike Galardi lament your incompetence and impotence (indeed your existence) over the years, I will say this: If Mr. Gentile accomplishes the seemingly impossible, and finds a way to save you, he deserves his own showroom at the Mirage, for he has just demonstrated the greatest magic trick ever witnessed by man.

*Editors note: The Mirage might want to prepare that show room. Although Lance Malone was convicted of wire fraud and conspiracy in the San Diego portion of the Operation G-sting trial, he was cleared of the most serious of the charges: bribery. Malone has received a sentence of three years, and a fine of $7,500. The Las Vegas portion of the trial has yet to begin. Malone's conviction, of course, is on appeal.*

*"There is no calamity greater than lavish desires.*
*There is no greater guilt than discontentment.*
*And there is not greater disaster than greed."*
*- Lao-tzu*

# MIKE GALARDI

*M*ike Galardi, the (now former) owner of Cheetahs Topless Club Las Vegas, Cheetahs Totally Nude, San Diego, and what had been the largest, most expensive topless club ever built; Jaguars Las Vegas, wasn't always the conceited, inconsiderate, asshole I make him out to be.

In 1991, when I first met Mike Galardi, he was opening his first Las Vegas strip club: Cheetahs.

The place had been a Hispanic dance club: The type of place you pick up the body parts and straight razors at the end of the night. The type of place that at first glance could have passed for Krispy Kremes during the frying hour for all the cop cars parked out front in response to calls.

Mike took the club—a failed experiment in the center of a deserted industrial area; no parking, no easy access, no drive-by business—and turned it into (arguably) the best known name in strip clubs on the planet. He achieved this feat the same way all small businesses achieve success; hard work.

Mike Galardi was the type of owner who would come into the club several times a day and wipe down the bar, sweep the floors, do the breakage, take out the trash, pick the cigarette butts out of the urinals.... He would give the girls encouragement and compliments (and even sneak them tips form his own pocket on particularly slow days). Cheetahs was his club, he was proud of it, and he was determined to make it a success.

Unfortunately for Mike, a successful strip club draws a lot of attention, and is an easy mark; Police, health inspectors, fire inspectors, judges, lawyers, and finally politicians took notice of Cheetahs, and began lobbying for their own slice of the lucrative pie.

A cop, or health inspector, or fire inspector could make Mike's life easier by ignoring a violation here or there. Mike could return the favor by offering what he—a strip club owner—had access to. It was a simple barter system that nearly every small business owner is familiar with. The only difference is, a strip club obviously has much more to offer than, say, a family owned sub shop or a pizza joint.

We never really considered them bribes, the gratuities heaped upon the city regulators of Cheetahs. Mike would simply say, "Take care of these guys," and we would. Free drinks and comped lap dances (which Mike himself would pay for), were the most common form of "taking care" of someone.

It wasn't until the politicians got their hooks into Galardi that lap dances and cocktails failed to be enough. "You can't pay your rent with a free drink." Not that a politician would ever consider paying for their own drink at Cheetahs. It was only that they didn't consider a measly cocktail as part of their due.

It was when the politicians began receiving pay for their services as "lobbyists," or "advisors," when Mike Galardi began to change.

Mike always had the potential to be a prick: Being the son of a strip club mogul (Jack Galardi of Pink Pony, and Crazy Horse fame), Mike had grown up with a very distorted childhood: He was raised in his father's strip clubs, and it showed. No one had ever told him "no." His high school friends worshiped him. All access to booze and naked women. Is it any wonder?

All of a sudden Mike's new best friends were the politicians. They began following him around and sucking his hind tit like the obsequious groupies of a rock star.

Mike began to believe his own press. He was surrounded by nothing but glad-handers telling him how much they loved him and how much they would love to do for him. They took the money and they promised to make life easier for him.

Mike Galardi, by his own admission, is guilty, and responsible for his downfall. I don't believe he felt he ever had a choice.

Begrudgingly, I do understand his logic.

A strip club is the only business on the planet which must conform to a new set of rules and operating parameters each and every month. Every city council meeting the rules governing strip clubs change; Light touching between customers and entertainers. Moderate touching. No touching. Six inches away, twelve inches, six feet... Nothing showing below the areola of the breast. Nothing below the crease of the buttocks... A thousand feet from the nearest church, school, or other strip club establishment, one thousand five hundred feet, two thousand....

In a never ending dance of political pandering, the strip club must learn how to adapt to vaguely interpreted laws and regulations nearly daily. Is it any wonder a strip club owner breaks down and begins paying the politicians to simply leave the laws unchanged, if nothing else? Wouldn't you? Or would you rather your business be torn asunder by the overwhelming bureaucracy heaped upon you by the local government?

If a politician came to you and offered to make your business more profitable, wouldn't you take the opportunity? Maybe not. Maybe it's just me.

Actually, I had the chance just recently to confirm that apparently, it would only be me (and Galardi) who would take the opportunity to "go along to get along."

A San Diego news anchor contacted me for an interview about my relationship with Mike Galardi, Cheetahs, and the whole mess of Operation G-sting. I proceeded to confuse her beyond words with my explanation on how I believed, though Mike Galardi had confessed to bribing public officials, that didn't necessarily make him a bad person. (Turning his back on those loyal to him makes him a bad person.) She had no comprehension what I was talking about, and accused me of "talking out of both sides of my mouth."

At first her statement angered me. Then I realized there are still people who believe in honest politicians, and operating a business just like it says in the business books. I am also aware that I am hopelessly out of touch with the mainstream and the political correctness of society. I still find it interesting that a news anchor, someone who has seen so much of life and society, could be so out of touch with the reality of the strip club business.

After about thirty minutes of trying to make my point, I surrendered. She didn't want to hear anything about how, before the politicians got hold of him, Mike Galardi had been a hard working, generous small-businessman.

What she wanted to hear was that Galardi was a mix of Stalin, Pol Pot, and Vito Corleone. She wanted to hear that he was a criminal mastermind worthy of being charged under the Patriot Act. I refused to tell her that because it's not the truth.

The truth is, Mike Galardi was never that important.

At worst, Mike is an asshole.Then again, so am I. So are most of you, and most of your friends (just ask your ex).

No one wants to believe that the FBI spent more than two years, and god knows how many millions of dollars, reiterating what most of us already know: Politicians are assholes too. No one wants to believe that the Federal government would use the Patriot Act to prosecute an American small-businessman—asshole. I know I don't want to believe it.

## FRIENDS

There is nothing like having the FBI raid your clubs to discover who your true friends are. Mike Galardi had that opportunity, and he came away with a friend. One.

Don't laugh. Try having the Federal government take everything you own, turn your life upside down, and charge you with the Patriot Act, and then look around yourself. Who would be left by your side?

Rich stood by Mike Galardi. For better or worse, he stands by him today. I truly hope Mike recognizes and appreciates it.

I worked with Rich from the very beginning of Cheetahs Las Vegas. He, like all of us, has his faults (yes, he's an asshole too), and we haven't always agreed, but we had some good times.

In the beginning, we would open the doors at 12:00 noon. Rich (bartender/manager) would set up the bar, I (DJ/bouncer) would put on an album, and we, along with all three or four of our entertainers, would sit at the bar eating Denver omelets, watching whatever game was on TV, and swapping lies.

The first customer would wander in about three in the afternoon, and wind his way down the long zig-zag hallway, blinking against the near total darkness of the club.

We would see him coming, and spring into action: I would jump into the DJ booth and begin a rambling dissertation about the merits of the girl who would climb onto the stage and begin spinning around the pole. The remaining girls would escort the customer to his seat at the bar and make him feel welcome.

It went on like that for many months, until eventually, the customers began coming in a little earlier, and the number of entertainers the "crowd" could support grew from three or four, to six or seven.

Rich was there at the beginning, and he was there at the end. As near as I can tell, he was the only one. I suppose, if nothing else, at least Mike Galardi now knows, without a doubt, who his true friends are.

## THE OTHERS

At one time, Mike carried no less than a dozen "managers" on his coattails, They were mostly useless sorts who couldn't hold any other job, or leeches who could offer perks. These store-bought friends were nowhere to be found after Mike was indicted and could no longer afford to support them.

The bitch of it is, there were those who would have been loyal to Mike to the end if he had only given them the chance. There were those of us who felt we owed him because of the living he afforded us, and because we felt he was worth our loyalty.

It is a shame he never recognized that fact until it was too late.

There may be a lesson in all this. If you know what it is, write me and let me know.

*"Keep your friends close, and your enemies closer."*
*- Sun-tzu*

*"Only two things are infinite, the universe and human
stupidity, and I'm not sure about the former."*
*- Albert Einstein*

## CABDRIVERS

### THE NEW VEGAS MOB

*Author note: I use the terms bribe, extortion, and
kickback, interchangeably throughout this chapter. They
are not the same. However, as not to place blame on a single entity for what has become a tragic situation, I will mix
and match terms, and allow the reader to make up their
own mind as to who should shoulder the bulk of the blame.*

With all that has been mentioned about poor
service, strong-arm robbery, nightly beatings
and such, and with all the strip clubs in Las
Vegas, how does Cheetahs maintain its standing-room-
only business? That's easy: bribes.

The most important factor in gathering customers
for a Las Vegas strip club, other than the girls, are the cab
drivers. Kick the drivers back five dollars per customer
they drop off, and your club will be busy. Kick back ten
dollars per head, and your club will be packed. Kick back
a nickel more than your competition and you will have a

line out the door every night, and that is exactly what Cheetahs has done. A standard kickback to cab drivers for a top club, as I write this, ranges between twenty, and fifty dollars per head (depending how popular and off-the-beaten-path your club is). This amount has occasionally gone much higher in an insane bidding war that only the cab drivers could win. The cover charge at Cheetahs went from ten dollars for the average white male (the price of admittance varies for ethnic males as explained in the next chapter), to twenty dollars to cover the twenty-dollar kickback to the cab drivers. The other major clubs were forced to follow suit. When Cheetahs bumped it up to twenty-five dollars bounty per head, the result was nothing short of phenomenal for business.

Cheetahs had been sliding ever downward in volume and quality of its customer base for years. The self-indulgent, piece-of-crap movie *Showgirls* put Cheetahs on the map. However, *Showgirls* was a long time ago now, and you can live only so long off your fifteen minutes of fame. Many factors I have already discussed; inconsistent practices, abusive employees, lack of club upkeep...were all contributing factors to the downfall. Adding an extra five spot for the cab drivers turned all that around in a heartbeat.

[*When Cheetahs was paying $5.00 more than the competition*] Try getting into a taxi, or limo, for that matter, and asking to go to Crazy Horse Too, or Olympic Garden. See where you end up. First, your cab driver may try to tell you the club you asked to visit is a dump and you would never want to go there. If that doesn't convince you, the driver may tell you the club you requested has changed into a gay bar, has burned down, he doesn't know where it is, or any combination of lies to prevent you from choosing that particular club. ("Crazy Horse Too? That turned into a gay bar years ago then somebody burned it down, besides, I don't really even remember where it was.") If you insist, chances are the next time you look out your window, you will be looking at Cheetahs, the club that pays the biggest kickback. I have had customers tell me all these stories and more. I even have had a group of tourists tell me they had asked to be dropped at their hotel, Caesar's Palace in one example, and still ended up at Cheetahs.

Does this extortion money really mean that much to a cab driver? Watch the numbers add up. Four customers at twenty-five dollars per head is one hundred dollars. That is a kickback from the club in addition to the fair and toke. Five customers earns the driver a buck and a quarter ($125.00). Five customers is all that is legally allowed to be carried in any taxicab in Las Vegas, it says so right on the side of the cab. However, I have seen up to nine pile out of a regular four-door sedan taxi, and thirteen out of a van (it looked like a circus clown car) that was dropping off in front of Cheetahs. At twenty-five dollars per head, those cab drivers took their lives, and the lives of their customers, into their hands for a couple hundred dollars worth of bribe.

The most I have ever personally paid to a (limo) driver for a single drop was $675.00 For twenty-seven customers.

It seems to me a slippery slope, this practice of bribing cab drivers, and playing this game of one-upmanship with the cover and kickback above that of your competitors. Where does it end? If the club down the street decides to offer \$25.$^{25}$ per customer, never doubt that club will be the new busiest club in Vegas, and Cheetahs will be back to doing a feeble business (or forced to offer \$25.$^{50}$ per customer).

Is bribing cab drivers for customers necessarily a bad thing? Free market society, right? Normally I would say, no. In this case, I am positive it is a very bad idea.

The taxicab and limo drivers whom I have met while at Cheetahs are, as a group, among the lowest form of humanity to which I have ever been exposed. (To qualify that statement, know that I have also been in the U.S. Army, dealt with pimps and drug dealers, known lawyers and politicians, and catered to pro athletes and Hollywood celebrities of all types. I have spent some time guarding federal prisoners, and have spent time on the other side of those walls. I have been in the strip club business for twenty years.) Drivers will eagerly break the laws pertaining to their job, including coercing, lying to, and physically endangering their customers. Drivers will even take every opportunity to steal from the very club paying their kickbacks.

The vast majority of cab/limo drivers I have dealt with will attempt to add at least one customer to their total when they return to get paid for a drop. That is, if a driver drops off three customers, he will tell the doorman he dropped off four. If he dropped four, he will claim five. It matters little to the driver that you watched, and counted, his customers as they exited the taxi. As far as a cab driver is concerned, it is always worth a try. After all, what can you (the club) do?

Cab drivers in Las Vegas enjoy the same protection as police, in that it is a felony to physically molest them—no matter what they do or how badly they might need it—and they take every advantage of that fact. More fearsome than that is their power as a group. If you try to ban a cab driver thief from your club, you run the risk of having every cab driver in the city boycott your establishment. Even major hotels have felt the sting of cab driver solidarity when one unlucky hotel was boycotted because the doormen at the hotel were loading limos full of customers for strip bar runs rather than letting the cab drivers get those customers. (Limo drivers regularly kick back half their take to the hotel doorman who loaded their strip club-bound customers.) During that boycott, customers of that major hotel could not get a cab for more than two and a half hours. Imagine the impact if drivers refused to drop at your topless club. Your business would literally be cut in half. For example: Once, during an early evening at Cheetahs, I caught a cab driver who would lurk around the side of the building and wait for customers, arriving in their own car, to enter the club. The cab driver would then approach and claim he had dropped the customers, and ask to be paid. When I refused to pay the driver for the bogus claim, the driver got on his taxi radio and announced to his cohorts that Cheetahs was no longer "cab driver friendly." I later learned there were cab drivers holding cardboard signs at the airport taxi stand claiming the same. We didn't get another cab drop at Cheetahs for nearly five hours. I should have been fired for that mistake.

The strip club war over taxi business actually

became a running joke for the doormen of these clubs after awhile. Every night when you reported for work, you would need to ask what the cover would be today; it could change that fast.

The owner of Cheetahs and the other major clubs once had a meeting, where each owner agreed on a set kickback amount to offer cab drivers so each club would be on equal footing. No more than a few hours after the meeting had concluded, Cheetahs bumped up their cab driver offering, taking advantage of the truce. Word spread quickly ("Well, Cheetahs is paying...") and the war resumed. It continues to this day.

It stands to reason that if the illegal practice of paying taxicab drivers to divert their customers from their intended destination were halted altogether, no club would have an unfair advantage, and each club would be forced to stand on its own merits. Strip club owner greed, and God knows what other asinine motivations, prevent this from happening. Moreover, it seems to me that when every club is paying the same amount for business, none has the advantage, and it is the same as paying no kickback at all—except, as mentioned, customers' lives are being endangered for that fee.

Where will it end? In my opinion, it will only end with one wrecked cab, a pile of a dozen dead tourists, and Las Vegas on the national media hot seat for "our" irresponsible behavior.

The cabdriver extortion issue has been recently revived in Las Vegas. A lawmaker in Carson City attempted to slip a bill through that would specifically outlaw the practice. (There are already unenforced laws against what the cabdrivers are doing.) The Governor wisely vetoed the bill. I say wisely, because leading up to the vote, the cabdrivers demonstrated their power by closing down the strip for a few hours with slow-moving, horn-honking cabs. They drove their point home with a threatened boycott of the airport if the Governor did not veto the bill. What was the Governor to do? A few hours of gridlock at the airport would shut down the city.

With the Governor too scared, and our mayor too wise to say boo to the cabdrivers, the cabbies have solidified themselves as the most powerful criminal force in Nevada.

*Editor note: This is a dynamic and ever-changing book (the hazards of printing current event titles). The deluge of mail we received from Las Vegas cabdrivers after the first printing, has motivated the author to add an amendment to this chapter.*

## THE BEST CABDRIVER I HAVE EVER MET

It seems I have done it again. It has been brought to my attention by countless, very vocal, very angry Las Vegas cabdrivers, that I have prejudged an entire group based on the actions of only the few thousand I have had personal experience with. I have lumped together an entire group of individuals without giving credit where it is due. I have, with my own mindless prejudice, failed to acknowledge a Vegas cabbie who has never—in our several year relationship—done me any wrong or harm. Moreover, this man has been a consistent friend to a friend of mine. To me, that is enough to qualify him as a good guy, and the best cabdriver I have ever met: Crazy Mike.

Crazy Mike has an interesting fetish: He likes to get beat up by women.

I was made aware of this particular cabdriver one day while I was doing my rounds through the VIP rooms at Cheetahs. I heard a loud slapping sound coming from the darkness of the front VIP room. It sounded like a slow, steady, yet exceptionally vigorous, clapping of the hands.

When I rounded the corner of the VIP room, I was treated to a sight, which honestly, if I worked the strip clubs for another twenty years, I could never become accustomed with. Crazy Mike was seated on a couch, blindfolded, his hands tucked politely beneath his thighs, and a young woman was slapping him across the face with all the strength she possessed.

A short distance away, the shift manager and the valet were watching, and doing their best to restrain their laughter.

I had no idea how to respond.

The manager silently waved me over and explained the situation: Crazy Mike would pay a girl several hundred dollars to beat the the living crap out of him. (I suspect he was tipping the manager a good deal also to allow it to happen on his shift.)

I couldn't appreciate the concept then, and I can't to this day, but to be fair, what gets me off probably doesn't do a thing for Crazy Mike, so who am I to judge?

Over the next several years, I had many occasions to watch over this activity. The manager would only allow it when the club was slow, and the VIP room was nearly empty.

I would stand guard, as much to protect customers from witnessing the act, as to insure none took advantage of a blindfolded man with a pocket full of cash.

At first it was only slapping. Eventually, the activity escalated.

One day Crazy Mike brought in a wooden paddle and asked that the girl beat his behind with it.

After that day, every now and again, Crazy Mike would come in to receive his well-paid-for beating. Afterward, he would limp his way back to his cab where he would lay down several layers of towels so he would not stain the seat with his blood.

To be sure, it was a rare girl who would concede to Crazy Mike's wishes, and she was always paid exceptionally well.

Crazy Mike was always polite, quiet, considerate, and never complained about the cabdriver kickback, even if the customers he brought were comped into the club, leaving him without payment. It just so happens he has a fetish that most people can't understand. Does that make him a bad person? Troubled maybe (you think?), but not bad.

So now I stand corrected, and the Las Vegas cabbies are vindicated: Crazy Mike is without a doubt the best cabdriver I have ever met.

*"Never try to reason the prejudice out of a man.*
*It was not reasoned into him, and cannot be reasoned out."*
*- Sydney Smith*

*"Nobody outside of a baby carriage or a judge's chamber*
*believes in an unprejudiced point of view."*
*- Lillian Hellman*

## RACISM

"*I*'m sorry there, bro, we have a dress code. You won't be able to come in tonight," the doorman recited the standard line to the confused customer.

"Since when? I come in here all the time," the customer, a black man in his twenties, gave the nearly standard reply.

"We don't allow three-quarter shorts," the doorman said, then looked past the customer to the other three black men standing just outside the front door, "or jerseys, or running suits, or baggy pants or those doo-rags." That pretty much covered everybody in the group.

Several other bouncers appeared, as if from the marble-tiled wall itself, to surround the increasingly agitated group of young, black would be customers.

As if on cue, a pair of young Caucasian customers exited the club. One of the whites was wearing a pair of three-quarter shorts of the same brand the deposed black man was wearing, and the other was wearing a San Diego Chargers football jersey with the name SEAU printed in bold letters across the back. The doorman sighed. The bouncers grinned.

"What about that?" The black customer wanted to know. "What about his shorts?"

"He must have got in before the shift change. The dress code starts at nine," the doorman lamely explained. No matter that it was now a quarter past three in the morning.

"This is bullshit!" One of the young black men finally shouted. "Y'all just a bunch of racists."

"The doorman sighed again, and the grins of the bouncers got even bigger. The bouncers moved closer to the group. Violence was near.

"Look," I said, "you guys know the deal. You're not stupid. Why don't you just go somewhere else?"

"Why, 'cause you don't let niggas up in here?" The customer asked in a flat voice that did nothing to restrain the venom. It was not truly a question.

"Now you got it," another bouncer said with a laughing tone.

We were close to coming to blows. The young black men would not want to lose face, but there were five of us surrounding them now, and in a fight, it wouldn't even be close.

I tried again, I'm not sure why. "Look, you guys are not getting in. You can fight us, or you can just walk away, but either way, you're still not getting in."

"You know what, fuck y'all white racist devils. You just ain't lettin' us in 'cause we're black." I could see the anger, the frustration in his face. I can still see it today.

"Put it up on the Internet, will ya? Save us some heartache," another of the bouncers taunted as the Cheetahs security crew moved forward. The black men backed away.

Vile verbal insults and taunts were thrown back and forth as the bouncers pushed their advantage, moving ever forward as the black men retreated. It was a potentially deadly adult version of the junior high school bully taking the smaller child's lunch money.

****

The situation described here happened, in some form, nearly every night I worked at Cheetahs.

It is Cheetahs policy to do everything possible to keep blacks and non-English-speaking Hispanics out of the club.

"Cheetahs policy! It's racist!" You scream. Yes it is. And your point?

"We reserve the right to refuse service to anyone for any reason" has been a blanket policy Cheetahs has hidden under since its inception. Apparently being a minority falls under "any reason." I have heard Mike Galardi—the Cheetahs owner—only half-jokingly state that he would like to put a sign at the front door that reads "No niggers allowed."

Are you offended by the term nigger? Good, you should be. It is an offensive term used to belittle and hurt. Take heart though, officially, Cheetahs doesn't refer to blacks, as niggers (not that you won't hear the word dozens of times a night at Cheetahs). Cheetahs owner and management, when in polite company, refer to blacks, and Hispanics, for that matter, as scumbags. Scumbags is an all-encompassing term for nonwhites (excluding Asians, who are just chinks in Cheetahsese).

But Cheetahs is a business, right? All money is green isn't it? There is no race on the almighty dollar. If this is your feeling, you make an excellent point, in the real world, but not so much in the strip club business. To Cheetahs, all customers are not created equal. The demographic most sought after and cultivated is the Caucasian male from thirty to fifty years old. These are the customers most strip bars love to see filling the establishment. Where do thirty-to-fifty-year-old Caucasian males like to go to spend their money? Anywhere there are plenty of young white women, and no young ethnic men. But then, I am telling you nothing you don't already know.

The upper-middle-class all-American Caucasian, who is so highly prized as a customer for the exotic entertainment business, is intimidated (or more accurately, outright terrified) by large groups of ethnic minorities. It is a simple fact that none but the most blind, sheltered or ignorant will attempt to deny.

In the 1980s it was the bikers who could ruin a topless club for their preferred demographic. After all, how many forty-year-old white businessmen would care to walk past a line of Harleys to enter a strip club? Not many, I can tell you from experience*. Now, in the new millennium, Harleys have become fashionable for upper-middle-class white men (they are nearly the only ones who can afford the status symbol bikes anymore), but the discomfort they feel around a group of minorities has not abated.

Why are these otherwise intelligent and sophisticated middle-aged white males intimidated when in a situation where minorities make up more than ten percent of a club's population? I have no idea. The fact is, they are, and it is never good for business to have your target customers feeling intimidated.

Am I attempting to justify the bigoted and racist acts of an entire business? If you feel stating a fact is justification, then I am. I am determined here to inflict the truth, and the truth is what it is.

Cheetahs has established set policies for eliminating "scumbags" that are as definitive as any the club has established on any subject to date. "Find a reason, any reason, to keep a scumbag out of the club" is a standing order that is followed with zest and enthusiasm.

Nearly all employees of Cheetahs are expected to show their disdain for scumbags whenever possible. Waitresses must ensure scumbags have a drink in their hands at all times. It doesn't matter if the individual in question has already fulfilled his two-drink minimum. If he is not currently purchasing, or in the process of finishing, a cocktail, that individual is targeted for eviction. The disc jockey's music selection must never venture into the realm of "Nigger music" (yes, that is the term for all rap and most R&B music at Cheetahs), that is, any song that might be enjoyed by a scumbag. Entertainers are told outright, when choosing their songs for their stage sets, that no rap or hip hop is allowed in the club as per the owner. If you have ever been in Cheetahs and have heard a long block of country or southern rock music, it was because the manager deemed that the club was too "dark": Too many dark skinned individuals in the crowd. The theory being that blacks have little desire to remain in a club that is playing country music. Is it effective? I couldn't tell you. I won't allow myself to think on it long enough to form an opinion.

If a scumbag seats himself at the bar, whether he is ordering drinks hand-over-fist or not, he will be targeted for eviction. The bartender cannot risk being seen catering to a scumbag by upper management, much less Mike Galardi himself.

When Cheetahs is standing room only and a good (white) customer need a seat, it is the scumbags who are targeted first for removal from a table. If the scumbag does not give up his seat quickly enough, or argues the point, he (they) will be forcibly removed, not only from the table, but from the club as well. In the case of Cheetahs, Ms. Parks' fight was for naught.

The most effective weapon Cheetahs maintains against scumbags, remains the front door. If the scumbag cannot get past the front door, the rest will take care of itself.

The dress code to enter Cheetahs varies depending on what the well-dressed young black man is wearing this year; Bandannas, headbands, doo-rags, backward baseball caps and Kangol-style caps are all examples of head gear that has made the list. Baggy jeans, jeans worn low on the hips, below-the-waist pants of any sort, three-quarter-length shorts, nylon pants or jogging suits of all description (even those eight hundred-dollar silk or velour outfits that would never see the outside of a nightclub). Any jersey (FUBU wear in particular) or oversized coat or jacket. All NFL team wear jackets (not just Raiders) are banned. "That's everything I own," I have heard one black man claim in astonishment. That is exactly the point.

When a black man or group of black men approaches the front door, the dress code is subject to change instantly. Whatever the trend or fashion in black clothing happens to be is what is currently banned by the club. Of course, this does not apply if the wearer of the clothes happens to be Caucasian, which is often the case.

Justifying again, but to put it into perspective, imagine me, a forty-year-old white male entering a nightclub on Martin Luther King Boulevard in any city in America. How would I be received (would I make it out alive)? It doesn't make it right, but it does go both ways, and it is the truth.

For the scumbag dressed like a white man, there are other hurdles he must negotiate. For the standard local white man, the cover charge is twenty dollars. For the woman accompanied by the local white male, there is no cover. For the white man or woman who arrives by taxi or limo, there is a twenty-five-dollar cover charge for each (in difference to the cab driver bribe). For the scumbag, local or not, the cover charge goes up from there. Forty dollars is not an uncommon amount to charge a non-white attempting to enter Cheetahs. If the owner or a manager is within earshot, the cover can go even higher. One particularly bold doorman, a favorite with the club, would announce the scumbag cover charge was one hundred dollars. I doubt he ever got any takers.

There is nothing more endearing to upper management than the doorman who invents a reason to keep a scumbag from entering Cheetahs.

Does my use of the word scumbag anger you? Does it insult you? Does it make you sick? By now the word probably makes you feel the same way the word nigger, or spick, or wetback, or chink makes you feel, and that is good. You should be sick and offended and insulted. Changing the name doesn't change the intent, and Cheetahs shouldn't be able to get away with what it does, but we know the difference between "can't" and "shouldn't," don't we? If your disgust spurs only one of you to seek action against this atrocity, it was worth the thousands I offended.

Are bouncers racist? For the most part, knowing the ones I have worked with for twenty years, the answer is yes, but probably no more so than society in general. In this business, you work for someone else. It is not your club or your money. You do as you are told or you will be replaced by someone who will do what he is told. Justifying again? Call it what you will, but it is a rare and fortunately individual in this world who does not have to compromise at least some of his standards to earn his living. Or maybe it's just me. The truth is, outside of the club, left to their own devices, most white bouncers are probably less bigoted toward blacks than the average white man. This is evidenced in the fact that most bouncers are weight-training athletes or martial artists who train among, and depend upon, all races in their pursuits. There are no colors in the gym—possibly the only true bastion of racial equality.

It was one of the most heartbreaking moments of

my life, the day I felt obligated to explain to a mentor and friend (my Brazilian Jiu Jitsu instructor), the policies on black men entering Cheetahs. My friend's father is black, and by accepting the Cheetahs policy, even in the pursuit of my living, I offended and disrespected a friend. This is a man whom I respect as much as anyone I have ever met. It is a heinous act for which there is no excuse. I will never forgive myself. I only pray that he can.

　　*An event which the power of perceptions and demographic response was illustrated, rather painfully, was when Barry (general manager), had the brilliant notion that he would hold a bike wash in front of Cheetahs one Saturday afternoon. The idiotic event took place shortly after Mike Galardi had bought his first Harley, and subsequently each manager also had to purchase a bike so he could accompany Mike on his rides (hysterically pathetic, actually. You should have seen the time Mike bought a racing go-cart). There were thirty motorcycles parked outside of Cheetahs from about noon to five in the evening. In that time there were exactly forty-one customers in the club. The same forty-one customers (the owners of the bikes and their dates) sitting around doing basically nothing. They had drank their fill hours earlier (before they got to Cheetahs) and they had no interest in buying lap dances. No other customers braved the imposing line of thirty bikes parked on the sidewalk along the front entrance. As you might imagine, it was not a banner day. Chalk another one up to the knowledge and skill of the Cheetahs management staff.*

*If a man defrauds you one time, he is a rascal;*
*if he does it twice, you are a fool.*
*- Author Unknown*

# FRAUD

"*A*ll right, everyone check your drawing tickets. It's time to give away the custom snowboard."

The majority of the crowd was there for the Harley-Davidson motorcycle that had been prominently displayed on the main stage for the past several weeks. The drawing for the bike would come last. The consolation prizes were going first.

"Okay, the number is..." The DJ made motions as if he were rummaging through the beer pitcher where all the ticket stubs had been placed. He withdrew an empty hand and read the preordained number. "Zero, zero, nine, three, five, one," the DJ announced. He looked around the crowd at the customers busily sorting through their raffle ticket stubs, hoping for the lucky number.

The DJ repeated the number and a heavyset drunk patron waddled up to the booth. "That's me," the shill belched.

"All right, we have a winner of the custom snowboard!" The DJ announced. The shill passed his ticket stub to the DJ, who dropped it on the mixing board with its matching half, the half that had been sitting on the board with the other winning tickets since before the drawing had begun. The customer went back to his seat to continue drinking his comped pitchers of beer. The snowboard stayed in the DJ booth. It was going home with the DJ.

Of all the prizes that were being given away, not a single one had actually been drawn for. Each and every drawing prize would be going home with the owner's friends, managers and Cheetahs employees. The manager made sure of it long before the drawing began. Winning ticket stubs were given to the winners days earlier. The matching stubs were given to the DJ. The DJ would simply call the numbers, and the winners would come up to the booth and claim their prize. In the case of the custom snowboard, the DJ had begged and pleaded and finally succeeded in procuring it for himself. A reliable friend of the manager had been given the winning ticket stub in exchange for all the free beer he could drink (the DJ would be charged employee prices for the beer, but it was well worth it). The shill customer would claim the prize when the number was called to make the show more believable, and simply forget to take it home, leaving it for the DJ.

The Harley-Davidson would be given away in the same manner, only there was no way an employee was getting his hands on that. The Harley was going home with Mike Galardi himself.

\*\*\*\*

All the drawings and promotional giveaways I ever presided over in Cheetahs had been perpetrated in this manner. A legitimate customer would never walk away with anything for free, not from this club. If you have any doubts about this, go to a Monday Night Football show at Cheetahs some time and watch the table closest to the back VIP room for a scrawny goateé wearing, long haired individual with his table piled high with promotional items. That has got to be the luckiest man alive. With all the autographed sports gear he has been given over the years, he could probably open his own sports regalia shop by now.

Not getting a fair shot at something for free is one matter, not getting what you are paying for is another altogether.

If you think that is Dom Perigon you just paid three hundred dollars for, you have a surprise coming. I have personally witnessed each general manager, and Mike Galardi himself, on many occasions, fill empty Dom bottles with Monet champagne, a much cheaper version of the bubbly wine. If you are crazy enough to order champagne at Cheetahs you will notice the bottle always arrives open or obviously re-corked. The cocktail waitress pours the champagne, and nobody is the wiser. The question isn't so much how they get away with it, but why they would even try.

A bottle of Dom Perigon costs the club about eighty dollars, a little less when it is purchased from the employee selling it out the back door of the local liquor warehouse store. At a retail price of three hundred dollars per bottle, the club is already making better than three hundred percent on the markup. Refilling the empty Dom bottles with cheaper champagne might save sixty dollars per bottle. Sixty dollars. Why would you risk your liquor license, that makes your club millions of dollars per year, for such a meager additional profit? I honestly have no idea. It is one of the most ignorant and obnoxious acts I have ever seen a bar owner perform. Not only are you risking your entire business for an extra sixty dollars, but you are outright cheating the highest-end customer you have.

Champagne sales are not the only method Cheetahs uses to bilk its customers. If you are seated with an entertainer with a glowing pink wrist band, it signifies that the entertainer is under twenty-one and it is illegal for her to consume alcohol. When the customer offers to buy the entertainer a drink (it is expressly against club rules for any entertainer to turn down an offered drink), the entertainer is supposed to order a "cocktail light." A cocktail light is code for, bring me a nonalcoholic beverage and present it like it is a regular drink (including charging the customer full price for the cocktail). A rum and Coke light is a plain Coke. A sea breeze light is a cranberry juice. A kamikaze light is a shot of lemon lime soda...you get the idea. It is troublesome to me, how the Alcohol Beverage Control (ABC) allows this to take place. It seems this would constitute fraud. If the entertainer is being served an actual cocktail containing alcohol, it is serving a minor. There doesn't seem to be a third option.

It is extremely petty and hazardous, to the hundreds of people the club employs and supports, to so recklessly defraud customers, and to what end? A few cents extra profit here and there? Does that mean so much to a multi-million-dollar business? Apparently so. I guess if I knew so much, I would be the millionaire.

The liquor stock room of Cheetahs is a veritable "don't do" list of liquor violations; marrying (pouring together) several partial bottles of liquor, using generic brands in place of name brands on the liquor guns, substituting one liquor for another without making it known...it goes on and on. The violations I have witnessed even include filling used bottled water bottles with tap water for resale. (No one outside Cheetahs will ever believe this. I can barely believe it myself, and I saw it happen!)

Good luck with that super-premium cocktail you ordered, and paid eleven dollars for. The bartenders are heavily discouraged (read; "I'll fire you if I catch you doing it") from pouring brand-name liquors when they can get away with substituting a cheaper brand or generic. You will be charged for the Kettle One, or Chevas, or Sauza (or whatever), but there is about a ninety-five percent chance you are drinking something else, or at least a mix. I have been told by one long-time bartender at Cheetahs that he had not poured a drink from his premium liquor bottles in over five years.

So how can you avoid being taken by this fraudulent behavior? First, know that any giveaway or raffle prize is going to wind up with a friend of the owner or management. Avoid shots of any sort bought for someone else. Know that employees cannot, under club rules, turn down an offered drink. Know also that employees, other than legal-age entertainers, are not allowed to drink alcohol on the job (at this writing, you may dance at Cheetahs starting at eighteen years old). Any alcoholic beverage you purchase for an employee is subject to being a fake. One general manager used to keep a Jagermeister bottle filled with cola for when a customer was generous enough to offer to buy him a drink. The GM may well have been fat, with rotting teeth, but he was seldom drunk. Don't ever purchase champagne of any sort. If you think you can out-smart the club management by requesting to open the bot-tle yourself, you may well end up with an already opened three hundred dollar bottle of bubbly being presented at your table. If you refuse to pay for the opened bottle, you will more than likely find yourself on the receiving end of a beating and a police citation for refusing to pay for a non-returnable item.

Another form of fraud that has the potential to cost you a great deal more than money, is lap dance fraud.

Brought on by slimy, greedy bouncers, and unscrupulous entertainers, lap dance fraud is a dangerous game that I truly don't see much of a solution for. It works like this: An entertainer performs three lap dances for you. She asks you for one hundred dollars. You can add, and you tell her you only got three dances, that equals sixty dollars—twenty dollars each. The entertainer runs to her slimy bouncer and tells him you owe her another forty dol-lars. The bouncer leans on you until you pay the extra forty. The bouncer keeps twenty, the entertainer keeps the rest.

I know this scenario sounds painfully familiar to many Cheetahs patrons. It happens every day, far more often than I would like to admit. It is a major reason enter-tainers and strip club bouncers have the reputation they do—as lowlifes.

Part of the problem lies with customers who try and

short entertainers for dances they actually received, causing honest entertainers and honest bouncers to be wary of all customer claims. Part of the problem lies with human nature; greed and laziness. Much of the problem lies with the fact that there is little recourse outside of back-alley justice for customers who cheat entertainers. And much of the problem lies with Cheetahs management turning a blind eye to the abuse of the unscrupulous entertainers and slimy bouncers.

The dilemma is, if you refuse to back your entertainers when they are robbed of their services, entertainers will leave, and your club will fail. If you allow bouncers to retrieve payment by any means necessary, some will take advantage and use it as a catchall to cover their criminal activity.

I don't know the answer to this problem. Just know that it happens.

At Cheetahs, unless you drink bottled beer exclusively, and have one or two entertainers whom you trust for your lap dances, it is extremely difficult to say with any confidence what exactly it is that you are paying for.

*"It's an awful thing to hear a strong, desperate, fat man scream incontinently in a cave at daybreak."*
*- O. Henry*

*"I think she really likes me."*
*- Anonymous*

# CUSTOMERS

## "TWO FAGS"

### A SHORT STORY

he first deep drag on the cigarette was tainted with sulfur from the freshly lit match as it was held to the end of the fag. The young man coughed a bit and spat a little something off the tip of his tongue as the hot smoke seared his lungs. He settled back in his seat and took another hit. He only smoked when he was drinking, or sometimes after sex, when the girl was. It seemed a combination of the two that had caused him to light up now.

The young man was not past his mid-twenties, dressed in the obligatory silk shirt, baggy slacks and funky platform shoes; a style that dominated the rave clubs of late.

The packed topless lounge buzzed around him with restless energy, as Darren played with the cigarette between his fingers and adjusted his crotch again, searching for a more comfortable position for his still-aroused condition. Mark sat opposite Darren at the small table and sipped a bottled water. He was about the same age as Darren, dressed nearly identically, and carried a replica demeanor as he reclined in his seat and tried to look cool.

"Man, that chick was all over me. She dug me," Darren said as he cupped his cigarette for another drag and flicked some ash.

"Yea," Mark asked, "what'd she do?"

"Dude, she did everything. She was grinding on me, biting on my ear...said she wanted to fuck me." Darren rolled his neck as he tapped the cigarette on the edge of the ash tray and recounted the story of his recent lap dance.

"No fuckin' way! She said she wanted to fuck you?" Mark asked in disbelief.

"Fuck yea she wanted to fuck me. Bitch was hot. Had her hands all in my shirt and shit, grabbing on my nipples, playing with my ring." He rubbed his sore nipples through his shirt. "She would probably have fucked me right there if the bouncer hadn't been watching." Darren smiled in memory and adjusted himself again.

"No shit! So you gonna hook up?" Mark asked.

"Hell yea, she said she would meet us for breakfast later. She has to make a couple hundred more first," Darren explained.

"Oh hell yea! Do you think she's got a friend?"

"I'm sure she does. You know I'll hook a brother up." Darren wedged the cigarette between his lips and gave Mark a high five in celebration of the night to come.

\*\*\*

The dressing room was nearly frantic with preening young entertainers in various states of undress. Deanna sat at her usual spot at the dressing table and dropped the lighter back in her bag. She would have to quit smoking one day, but it wouldn't be today—not with the jerk-off customers she was dealing with tonight. Kelly, a svelte beauty, sat in the seat next to Deanna and waved her hand at the smoke trailing from her friends cigarette.

"Sorry about that baby," Deanna said as she moved the ashtray with her cigarette to her opposite side, away from Kelly.

"Tough night?" Kelly wanted to know. She was still applying a pair of eye lashes that could have doubled as a peacock tail, and hadn't been out on the floor yet.

Deanna scoffed her acknowledgment. "Both types out there tonight. The single and lonely, and the married and sad. Nobody wants a dance,. Everybody wants to take you out."

"That's the way it always is. They're going to take you out and spend all this money on you, but they're too cheap to buy a lap dance," Kelly said.

"No doubt," Deanna agreed. She took a dainty hit off her cancer stick and blew the smoke up and away from Kelly before she continued. "You should have seen this kid I just danced for. Good looking, about twenty-five, kind of short. I'm dancing for him and he keeps trying to stick his tongue in my ear. I had to yank his nipple ring, like twice, just to get him to stop."

"Great," Kelly groaned. "I don't even know why I

showed up tonight."

"Cause you got rent."

"No doubt," Kelly conceded. "God, I hate guys like that. Nipple rings creep me out. It's like they are just waiting for someone to tell them they are gay so they can stop pretending."

"I don't think this guy was gay," Deanna said. "He almost came in his pants when I said I wanted to fuck him."

"Eew, really?"

"Yea, I had to get off him for a minute. He was like 'Oh, baby, fuck me, yea, do it.'" Deanna moaned the vulgarities in imitation of her previous customer, and both girls laughed.

"That bullshit always works. Guys are so stupid."

"He thinks I'm going to breakfast with him."

"Yea, anyway...."

Deanna laughed along with Kelly, and took another drag off the fresh cigarette.

\*\*\*

He blew the smoke up in the air and watched the flashing multicolored lights reflect off the tendrils. "I told her I was Robert Rodriguez."

Mark snorted on a little water that had gone up his nose at that. "You told her you were Robert Rodriguez? Shit, you're not even Mexican."

"I'm half," Darren protested. "Besides, I don't think he is either. I think he's from Texas or something ."

"You don't even speak any Spanish," Mark said,

laughing.

"So? she's just a fucking stripper, she wouldn't know the difference."

"Good point. So who am I supposed to be, Quentin Tarantino?"

"You're ugly enough to be," Darren said.

"Suck my dick, nigger," Mark said, doing his best Tarantino impression. They both laughed.

\*\*\*

"Robert Rodriguez?" Kelly wanted to know. "*The* Robert Rodriguez?"

"Yea, I mentioned I was an actress, and he comes up with that. Like I wouldn't know Robert Rodriguez if I saw him. First of all, the guy's about six inches too short. That, and I don't think he even speaks any Spanish. I asked him how old he was in Spanish and he just looks at me like he doesn't know what I'm saying." Deanna scoffed at the thought, took a long drag from her dwindling cigarette and placed it in the ashtray.

"Everybody's got to be somebody, right?" Kelly stated rhetorically.

"No doubt. This guy's a real jerk-off though. Tells me he's this big movie director, then says he wants to go to breakfast with me and discuss my part in a movie." Deanna shook her head sadly.

"Yea, like it's the first time anyone has ever tried that one on you, right?" Kelly scoffed.

"Right."

"Once I had this guy tell me he was Oliver Stone,"

Kelly said.

"Fat guy, wrinkled blue suit, old, stringy hair, no shoes, so messed up he couldn't hardly stand, came in about a month ago?" Deanna wanted to know.

"Yea," Kelly confirmed.

"That *was* Oliver Stone," Deanna said.

"Oh," Kelly said, "whatever, I don't want to be in the movies. The guy was cheap anyway."

"Like it's going to impress us anyway," Deanna said. "I don't care who you know or who you blow, as long as Ben Franklin is doing your talking, I'm listening."

"No doubt," Kelly agreed. "So you going back out there or what?"

"Oh, hell no." Deanna coughed, blowing smoke from her stub of a cigarette into Kelly's face, then waved it away in apology. "I've made my money. Besides I told that moron I would go to breakfast with him. He'll just be following me around like a little puppy dog for the rest of the night."

"Does he have any more money?" Kelly wanted to know.

"I think so," Deanna said. "He got like a thousand dollar cash advance, and he only gave me like three—cheap fucker."

"So where did you say he was sitting again?" Kelly asked.

Deanna snubbed out her cigarette and grinned.

\*\*\*

"So is she coming back out or what?" Mark was

getting restless.

Darren looked toward the dressing room. "Yea, chicks take a long time getting dressed you know?" He took a final drag on his cigarette and wrinkled his face in repugnance. The filter smoldered at the base of the fag. A beautiful young woman sauntered up and welcomed herself to a seat on Darren's lap.

"Hi, I'm Kelly." The young woman said snuggling onto his crotch. "You look familiar. Aren't you a famous movie director or something?"

Darren crushed the butt into the ashtray and looked into the smiling eyes of the woman on his lap.

* * * *

Classifying customers as a single type would be as difficult and ignorant as attempting to classify entertainers.

Customers come in all ages, shapes, sizes, color, creeds...and most of all, needs. To lump them together as "the type of guy who would hang out in a topless bar," shows as much bigotry and prejudice as making a determination about a person based on his skin color or religious preference. Don't be disheartened if you still hold that there is something wrong with the type of guy who would hang out in a topless bar. We all show prejudice in some manner, this may simply be yours.

Life in a strip club is life distilled to its essence. You see the worst, and best, of human nature without the heavy veils of political correctness that normally obscures the truth in the real world. To hear a customer state, "You look just like my daughter. Would you like to dance for me?"

Illustrates one extreme, while witnessing a young woman tolerate society's scorn and hypocrisy so her child might live a better life than she had opportunities for, illustrates the opposite.

Customers are not all lecherous old perverts looking to cheat on their wives and squander fortunes that might have been spent on their children (though some nights, I swear, it feels like that). The truth is, a customer, whether his wife will ever accept the fact, or if he himself will admit to it or not, is in need of much more than sexual arousal when visiting a strip club.

Based on twenty years of observation, it is obvious to me that sex is not the prime motivating factor for a man to spend his money on a young, virtually naked woman in a strip club (though even the customer may protest that it is).

The main motivation for the customer lies in the acceptance and caring he may lease, at least for a moment, from another human.

Acceptance? Caring? From a stripper?! Indeed.

A man works a forty-hour week. He receives few accolades and is appreciated even less. His co-workers snipe and pick and bitch and whine continually. His teenage children look upon him as a sodded old fool. His wife has too many of her own problems to care—even if she found the energy—and to her, he could never broach the subject of his needs. A man sometimes needs to feel powerful, dominant, needed. The company he works for existed before he came along, and will continue to exist after he is gone. His children have their own friends. His wife has been taught by society that it is shameful to lean on a man for total support. He is left with few methods of expressing his nature—what nature originally intended—of a powerful provider, a dominant being.

Enter the strip club: A man may rent the attention of a young woman; a woman ostracized by society, more innocent than himself in the ways of the world. A young woman who depends on his generosity, his ability to provide. For this ability, he is blessed—for a few minutes, or a few hours—with what he needs most: the feeling of being needed, of virility, of power—the root core of primal man—which, despite the attempted socializing out of this condition, is an integral, inherent part of all men.

For only a few (or a few hundred) dollars, he is transformed. He is attractive, he is powerful, he is virile and compassionate and interesting. Every word from his lips is a treasured gem of wisdom. His body is a Greek god's temple. He is *Man*. More than a man, he is Conan the Barbarian. He is a superhero come to life. He is the only real man on the planet. No one else compares. His job of checking for typographical errors on his company's financial statements is the most fascinating concept the young woman, who devotes her entire attention to him and him alone, has ever heard. The body he had assumed was irretrievably out of condition is a continual source of pleasure for her gently wandering fingers. She understands and appreciates things even his wife cannot. Things that cannot be expressed to friends or co-workers (they have their own problems) are absorbed and accepted by the young woman who dotes on him, and him alone. How can he tell his wife of twenty years he feels impotent in life: his dreams are faded, his strength is gone? He can tell this young woman, and she consoles, accepts, vindicates. She convinces him that he is important, strong, virile, needed—at least by her, at least for the moment—and often that is enough.

It's either that, or it's just to become sexually aroused.

If it were only sex a man wanted, he has innumerable ways of procuring that, even if simply paying a prostitute for a moment of release. A prostitute will certainly fulfill a man's need for physical sexual release, but there will be little nurturing or emotional support. The prostitute will not speak with him or make him feel needed.

If you believe all this should be obtainable from a partner—a wife—please remember, "should" and "are" are two different concepts, the truth of which is inflicted upon us throughout our lives. Daily, we are assailed with the difference between "should" and "can't." Between "should" and "is." Between "should" and "are." One can go through life with closed eyes and deny it. One can fight it, or one can accept it, and learn from it.

Would anyone truly expect a wife or husband to be able to maintain the level of attention and nurturing necessary to keep a partner completely satisfied throughout their entire lives? Women are indeed powerful, mystical creatures, but what you would be asking would tax a god. (Indeed it could be said that God is incapable of this feat much of the time.) What of *her* needs, her exhaustion, her frustrations, her desire to be desired? For every couple whom you can name who are able to maintain that level of nurturing and attention, there are tens of thousands who cannot. That makes that one fortunate couple the anomaly. To base the expectations of an entire culture on an anomaly seems less than fair. A surrogate to fulfill your needs is not a sin. It is simply human.

Female customers in the traditional strip club have become routine and commonplace in the past few years. Whether it's because of a newfound sexual awareness, Hollywood's influence, or the examples of the performing artist Madonna, is beyond me. (I'm thinking Madonna.) What is notable, is that married, heterosexual women have discovered the pleasures of the female entertainer strip bar, and are flocking to these establishments in astonishing numbers.

A woman does not need to be overtly bisexual to enjoy the attentions of a beautiful woman. Much like their male counterparts, a female customer can find acceptance and an elevated sense of self-worth through these attentions. A woman with four children who imagines herself sixty pounds overweight, who hasn't felt attractive to her husband, or men in general for years, is admired, doted upon, caressed, made love to (in a figurative sense) by a beautiful young woman. An attractive person sees her as attractive, as desirable, as sexy. All this need not be sexual, but simply self-esteem building.

A cheap method of building one's self-esteem, you complain? A false sense of self-worth, paying a young woman to give you the attention you crave? And your point?

Is the feeling you receive from an exotic entertainer any less valid than that which you earn in other ways? You raise an award-winning child (and advertise the claim on the bumper of your car). You procure your raise at work. You receive accolades for your creations. You obtain a wealth greater than your neighbor's: These are all outside influences—peers, friends, society—bestowing you with a sense of self-worth, of pleasure, of pride. Is there any valid difference?

It is all fantasy. Paying a young woman to find you attractive, interesting, sexy is not real. It is a fantasy. Yes, it is a fantasy; like going to the movies and losing yourself for two hours in someone else's value system, someone else's life, that you wish (you fantasize) was our own (or celebrate is not). It is a fantasy; like going to the amusement park for an adrenaline rush to break the monotony of your daily routine. It is a fantasy. But if the feeling you get is the same, if your emotions and endorphins are elevated...where lies the difference?

Enough. I am no psychiatrist. I m a strip club bouncer, and these are simply the truths that have been inflicted upon me.

Least you believe all topless bar customers are as inert as the examples given above, know that there are some customers, men and women alike, who are drawn to strip clubs, and exotic entertainers, for purely malicious reasons. These are people who feel so impotent in their lives, so frustrated in that impotence, that they must inflict discomfort and pain upon others. The only people they feel confident (safe) in assailing with their malice are those they are paying to withstand their abuse. A man who is frustrated with his job, his wife, his kids, his life, feels he can vent his pain on a stripper: a young woman without the support of "decent" society. Who ever heard of a stripper winning a sexual harassment complaint? A man may feel he may verbally abuse a young woman in this profession with legal impunity.

A successful exotic entertainer looks upon this type of customer with pitying eyes. It is a poor, pathetic, small person who has no other avenue for the rage bottled in his damaged soul than to target a stranger—a young, greatly defenseless stranger—who has enough of her own problems to deal with, without being set upon by an angry, bitter loser. This type of customer feels he has paid for the privilege of abusing this stranger, this exotic entertainer.

Be forewarned; if you are this abusive individual of which I speak, your abuse may be invisible to the legal system, but it is not invisible to me, and those like me. I am betting, not to God either.

The mental abuse the typical exotic entertainer takes daily in the course of her job would crush a woman, or man, in another profession. Women nationwide complain of men making comments about their appearance, or dress, or complain simply about the way they are looked at—the duration or perceived intent of that look. Men have lost their jobs, companies have been chastised, an entire society has been put on notice for these heinous sexual harassment infractions against women. Infractions that wouldn't even raise the pulse of an exotic entertainer.

Customers of the strip club are free from the fear of rejection, but more importantly, they are free from the oppression of political correctness. In the strip bar, "You've got great tits," is a compliment. In society, the same comment is cause for the destruction of a life.

I, no doubt, have been spoiled. I have spent the past twenty years in an environment where I could say what I felt, and express what is natural. An environment where the cupping of a buttock or breast (between employees) is akin to a handshake. An environment where you are asked for your opinion, an honest critique of a flawless naked body, and where you may give it, without tempering your language. I have no delusions about my ability to function in regular society at this point, twenty years later. I can certainly empathize with customers who enter the topless lounge for a few hours of relief from the politically correct oppression that has overtaken our society and our lives.

What makes a good topless club customer? It is not wholly dependent upon how much he spends (though it doesn't hurt). A good topless club customer has common sense. A good customer applies his common sense so he can keep what happens in the topless club in perspective.

Each topless club customer believes his situation is unique. The customer may well be unique. His situation is not.

I hear the same major complaints each and every night, and the majority of those complaints lack one thing: common sense. If the following sounds familiar to you, you may lack this common sense.

## I JUST GOT RIPPED OFF

"I just got ripped off," the red-faced customer frantically proclaimed the moment he was within ten feet of me.

My ears perked up, after all, I was security for the strip club. Nobody would be ripping off anybody. Not on my watch.

"Who was it?" I queried, scanning the club for suspicious looking characters. Maybe someone sprinting for the front door with the red-faced customer's wallet in hand.

"That girl right over there." Red-face pointed to 110 pounds of scantly clad curvaceous twenty-year-old beauty personified.

My ears deperked. "Really," I said, "and exactly how is that?"

The customer instantly recognized my change in tone and attitude. I could see the gears turning in his head, thinking of a way he could explain his dilemma without sounding like a total fool. It wasn't going to be easy.

"Well, we were sitting together, and I bought her two drinks..." The customers eyes shifted left, either remembering, or thinking up a lie, I can never recall which is which. I let him continue. "Well, I bought a dance, and I asked her...well, she said that...." Give a man enough rope and a shovel....

"Let me guess," I interrupted. I could tell his story better from this point than he could, anyway. "You asked her how much it would take to get her to go back to your hotel room, and she said something to the effect of; 'lets get some more dances and we'll talk about that later,' right?" I could tell I was nearly quoting word for word by the customer's expression and ever darkening color. "You probably gave her some money up front, maybe $250.00, to meet her at your hotel...?" I didn't get a response, but I knew I was right. I decided to give the customer an easy out. "Soliciting prostitution is illegal in Clark County, sir. So call a cop and explain it to him, or chalk it up as a relatively cheap lesson on how to behave in a strip club. Either way, go away." I shooed at the customer who wandered off, apparently satisfied with the "lesson".

\* \* \* \*

There is a ninety foot sign out front of Cheetahs that reads; Topless Club. There is a doorman at the front door checking ID's to insure everyone who enters is of legal age, and presumably an adult. There are strikingly beautiful, scantly clad twenty-year-old women sitting on overweight fifty-year-old men's laps. Is it a mystery what's going on here?

Still, I hear the "I got ripped off" complaint continually. Recently I even saw a headline in the local paper (attributed to a police officer) proclaiming that strip clubs are, "one big con game." Exactly who's getting conned here?

By its very nature and definition, everything that takes place in a strip club is fantasy. How else can you explain a beautiful woman, young enough to be your daughter, finding you totally irresistible? Ripped off? Conned? Give me a break.

You are paying for fantasy, she is providing that fantasy. It is an equitable trade, and no one is trying to trick you.

Even if the conversation goes into the illegal realm of sexual innuendo, or illicit promises that go unfulfilled, it is totally irrelevant. You are paying for a fantasy, that is what the strip club is for. That is why you came. No rational, sentient individual can possibly claim they have been duped under these circumstances. It can not be done.

I have been to Disneyland. I rode rides with names like "Space Mountain" and "Pirates of the Caribbean." Never once was I actually in space, or on a mountain, or saw a real pirate. Was I conned? Was I duped? Was I ripped off?

That day at the amusement park cost me about three hundred dollars with admission, lodging, food, and souvenirs. My wife and I stood in lines for about seven hours, for a total of less than thirty minutes worth of actual ride time. For that same three hundred dollars, my wife and I could have gone to the strip club, got a dozen lap dances (nearly an hour of "ride time"), made believe we were making love to a intensely sexy young woman who was dying to come home with us that night, and lived off that fantasy for weeks to come. Both the amusement park and strip club have their advantages and disadvantages for your entertainment buck, but I wouldn't call either one a con, a dupe, or a rip off.

Use a little common sense during your next visit to the strip club. It's a fantasy. Live it to its fullest. Then go home and relive it in your memory as many times as you like. If you would like to complain about being ripped off, duped and conned, tell me about how much you paid in taxes this year to liberate Iraq.

For those who lack common sense, or need a more direct guide to being a good strip club customer, I have included the following "Top Ten" list (henceforth putting an end to strip club ignorance once and for all).

## THE STRIP CLUB TOP TEN DON'T DO LIST

**10) Don't try and claim you didn't know you were getting a lap dance.**

If you are in a strip club, and there is a half naked woman on your lap, you are probably getting a lap dance.

Tens of thousands of times over the years (it seems like tens of thousands anyway) I have heard customers complain; "But I never asked her for a dance," to which I formulated a standard set of proofs:

Q: Was she on your lap?

A: Yes.

Q: Did she have her top off?

A: Yes

Q: Was the music playing?

A: Yes

Conclusion: You were getting a lap dance.

Think about it; you are in a strip club. A gorgeous twenty-something woman is sitting half naked on your lap. Exactly why do you believe she is there? (I think she really likes me!)

**9) Never ask an exotic entertainer on a date (or home with you) while she is working.**

A strikingly beautiful twenty-something woman generally doesn't have so much trouble meeting men that she needs to pay a strip club exorbitant amounts in house fees and tip-out for the privilege of meeting you.

**8) Never tell anyone how much money you spent in the club.**

Because you will become a target? No. Because no one cares. "I just spent three thousand dollars in this joint," is a common statement among disgruntled patrons being tossed out of the bar for one infraction or another. The first thought through a bouncer or manager's mind upon hearing this is, "How much of that do I get?" Do you truly believe anyone except the owner cares how much money you spent in the bar? (And you're not dealing with the owner.) The only thing worse is telling someone how much you would have spent if you weren't getting thrown out (useless information).

**7) Never openly criticize the looks of any of the entertainers.**

Have you looked in the mirror lately? Have you looked at your wife? What makes you think your opinion on how much a woman should weigh, how large her breasts should be, how big her back side is, etc....matters at all to anyone in a strip club? Don't like the looks of anyone here? Leave.

**6) Never try and sleaze your way out of the cover charge by any of the following claims:**

"I know the owner." (The owner doesn't have any friends without VIP cards.)

"We're going to spend a lot of money in there." (Why would the doorman care how much money you are going to make that cheap bastard multimillionaire who owns the joint?)

"You don't know who I am," or "I'm Joe Blow, the famous person." (Great, then you can afford the cover.)

**5) Never stop half way across the parking lot and shout back at the bouncer who just threw you out of the club; "I'm going to come back and kick your ass!"**

You come off looking like a punk. You just had an opportunity a moment ago. You should have done it then and saved yourself a trip.

**4) Never forget to tip your cocktail waitress.**

Yes, we know the price of a drink is outrageous in a strip club. It's not the waitresses fault. She didn't price the drink, and she doesn't get to keep the money. She just fought that mob surrounding you to get you that drink, show a little appreciation. (Try telling your wife to bring you a beer without saying thank you, see where that gets you.)

**3) Never, never, never, ask for a discount lap dance.**

Asking for a discount doesn't reflect on the quality of the entertainer. It reflects on you. (Go back to K-Mart where you belong.)

**2) Never claim you got scammed (or ripped off, or conned) by a topless entertainer.**

You're in a strip club for goodness sake. The girl is supposed to tell you all that good stuff. That's why you came, to hear all that good stuff. Of course it's a lie. That's the whole point. (Besides, if you got scammed, or ripped off, or conncd, you just admitted to being out-smarted by a twenty-year-old stripper.)

**1) Never, ever, under any circumstances, decline to pay for a lap dance.**

Even if you get away scott-free (no bouncer beating) you will have to look yourself in the mirror every day for the rest of your life knowing you are a thief. You stole from a beautiful young woman who had spent her time and energy making you feel good. (Is there anything lower? Not something you want to take to your grave.)

* * * *

Now you can feel free to enjoy the strip club as the pagan gods intended, without the blanket of ignorance your predecessors languished beneath. (No need to thank me, just knowing I could be of help is reward enough.)

# MURDER

*N*o clever story to start this chapter. No anecdote to make a point. I do not know how to tell this truth without sounding evasive, or worse, coy. I will simply state the events as I recall them.

Know that I am, ultimately, a survivalist in that I will do what I must to ensure the existence of my family and myself.

In 1995 I was interviewed by two Las Vegas Metropolitan Police homicide detectives who recounted to me this event:

A customer at Cheetahs had been seen arguing with a manager and an unnamed bouncer, about 9 p.m. That customer was beaten and dragged from Cheetahs by the manager and the bouncer. Once outside the back door, the manager proceeded to administer a beating that left the customer unconscious and helpless. The customer was left alone and unconscious, behind Cheetahs, until a gang of youths, who happened to be passing by, saw the unconscious customer, robbed and beat the customer to death.

The homicide detectives told me I had been witness to the beginning of these events, and that there were several witnesses to the fact that I had been severely distressed in the aftermath. The police detectives told me that they could protect me, in the event that I received death threats from Cheetahs ownership or management—if I wished to tell what I knew about what had happened that night.

Even though the FBI, for several years, had been claiming the club owners had ties to organized crime, I was told I would be protected from retribution if I wanted to turn anyone in for their part in this murder.

This is what I was told.

No one from Cheetahs has ever been charged for any crime in this matter as far as I am aware.

Again, Cheetahs is not alone or unique in this matter:

The same year, a neighboring strip club came under investigation for a murder outside the back door to their club. No one was ever convicted of that murder.

A couple years later, at the same club, a customer's neck was broken. No one was convicted in that case.

Just this year, a former doorman from yet another strip club was shot and killed for speaking badly of the club. At least two individuals related to the club owner have been charged with that murder. We will have to wait and see if there is a conviction in that case.

For those wagging their fingers and saying "I told you so," remember, you are more likely to be murdered in high school, than in a strip club.

*"It was written I should be loyal to the*
*nightmare of my choice."*
*- Joseph Conrad*

*"The wicked shall see it and be grieved: he shall gnash his*
*teeth and melt away: the desire of the wicked shall perish."*
*- Psalm 112*

# A SELF-INDULGENT RANT
## (AND WARNING)

*W*hat is the end product of twenty years in the environment with which you have just become familiar? I am, no doubt, a product of my choosing. I have chosen to live my life as I have, and I will not deny what I have become. You will make up your own mind about what you have read, and what the effects are on a man such as myself—but not before you are privy to this last revelation.

With all due credit given to cabdrivers, angry customers, corrupt politicians, incompetent management and nonsensical owners, there is one—the lowest of the low—who needs to be exposed before this story is finished. I am speaking of those who would take advantage of their charges—those they have sworn to defend.

A predator who preys on the weak, or helpless, or unsuspecting can be forgiven; it is in their nature, and nature is the most powerful of forces. Those who cannot be forgiven are those who prey on the ones who trust them: the predators who use their position as protector to exploit and use and corrupt: clergy who take advantage of the innocent. Police who use to ill advantage their indisputable power. Parents who abuse their children. And foremost (in my limited strip club world) strip club employees who exploit their entertainers.

There is, and I suspect always has been, a contingent of those who would take advantage of and abuse those who are the very reason for their employment. A strip club would not exist without willing entertainers. Managers would not be employed at a quarter-million dollars per year. Bouncers would be collecting shopping carts in the Wal-Mart parking lot if not for the strength of the entertainers that provide them with their livelihood. This is a simple fact that cannot be disputed.

There can be no lower form of human than one who takes advantage of a helpless, trusting individual who has put herself in his care.

I hear stories of bouncers and management extorting money from entertainers for any number of reasons. How could a man, any man, who accepts payment for protection, refuse to protect? A man could not. *A man could not.* I have known those who would deny a young woman the confidence and security she needs to perform her job, a job that in turn provides managers and bouncers with their own (very good) living.

Men who work at strip clubs are there for one purpose and one purpose only: to provide a safe environment for the entertainers to perform their jobs. That is all. If a man cannot, or is not willing to perform that one single task—for the money the club pays him—he has no business taking the job.

I never allowed these actions in the clubs where I worked. A man would have to be willing to take his life in his hands, or be willing to end my life, if he were to attempt to bargain for the safety of an entertainer.

There are many who do bargain and barter—refuse to perform their duties without added compensation. To those: I will meet you in hell, and there will be a reckoning.

****

In early summer 2003, probably the most distressing event of my nearly twenty years in the business occurred. In retrospect, it also was the most likely reason for my dismissal from Cheetahs.

## THE WORST THING I HAVE EVER SEEN

Twenty years as a strip club bouncer, over twelve of those years at Cheetahs Las Vegas, and yes, I've seen some shit. I have been witness to things that no man should ever be forced to witness.

When asked; what is the worst thing I have ever seen, and I am asked that question often, I used to pause, thinking of the tens of thousands of crimes and sins I have witnessed and partaken in: senseless violence, drug addiction, racism, strong arm robbery, political corruption, sexual assault... If it can be considered a crime or sin, chances are I've crossed its path, and called it my job.

I don't hesitate anymore when I am asked that question. What is the worst thing I have ever seen? Now I have a very definitive answer.

I was working the VIP room at Cheetahs when the Las Vegas Metropolitan Police Vice Squad made one of their frequent tours of the club. Two officers stood beside me, looking over the club and the VIP room. We exchanged meaningless banter about nothing in particular. There was the usual tension between the officers and myself: The officers blatantly loathe to be forced to converse with a lowly strip club bouncer, and myself, spewing the usual ego-stroking bullshit about how interesting a vice officer's job must be (compliments that could mean the difference between a ticketless night, or having half your entertainers cited for "lewd behavior"). Everything was going well. The officers seemed their typical lethargic selves, unwilling to crack the ticket book that close to the end of their shift (sloth is not always a bad thing), when one of the two officers exclaimed with wonder; "Oh man, look at that."

I turned, and the three of us were witness to an entertainer being sexually assaulted by a customer.

The customer had the entertainer by the buttocks with both hands, and was crushing her against him. He forced his face into her stomach. His vile mouth sucked at her skin.

The entertainer was fighting for her life, striking and clawing and pulling the customers hair. The intoxicated customer, much larger and stronger than the 100 pound woman, was heedless of her attempts to free herself. His fingers dug into her skin, and his lips and mouth and teeth, continued to violate her.

I sprinted across the room and proceeded to do what any man would have done in my position. I felt I needed to get my licks in quickly before the vice officers got to the man and finished him off. I might have beat the man to death—I was that offended and enraged—but for the vice officer who saved the customer's life, and not at all how you might imagine.

In mid-throttle, from behind, I heard the vice officer who had originally witnessed the assault, shouting at the victim of that assault: "How can you let that guy grab on you like that? What's the matter with you? That guy was all over you."

I forgot the customer, let him fall to the floor—crawl his way out of the VIP room and the club—and turned on the vice officer. The vice officer, a man (so I had thought) sworn to serve and protect, had the victim entertainer gripped tightly by the upper arm and was chastising her for all he was worth.

Mine was not a conscious decision, or in retrospect, probably even a rational one, but I am convinced it was the right decision. I forced the officer to release the victim and started in on a lecture of my own—to the officer. I can not repeat what I said. You would not want to hear it in any case. Just know, after nearly twenty years as a topless bar bouncer, I have been exposed to a great deal of vile language, and I used it all on the vice cops that night.

The two officers, after a brief and feeble retort, sulked from the bar with my infuriated and abusive language chasing them all the way to the parking lot.

The attitude displayed by the vice officers that night

is unforgivable. It is the same thinking that blames a woman's rape on her choice in clothing. The thinking has no place in any society, much less displayed by a public servant sworn to protect.

The memory haunts me to this day. Not because of the sexual assault by the customer (like I said, I understand the concept of predators), but because of the actions of the police officers that night. I will never forgive or forget those actions, and neither, I suspect, will the victim, or worse, the attacker.

The worst thing I have ever seen? A representative of our society, our civilization, blaming a woman for her own assault. At least now I have no fear of what I might witness in hell.

I have never been told the reason for my being fired from Cheetahs, but if this incident was a contributing factor, I accept my dismissal with pride.

*"Thus, in a real sense, I am constantly writing autobiography, but I have to turn it into fiction in order to give it credibility."*
*- Katherine Paterson*

*"Truth is more of a stranger than fiction."*
*- Mark Twain*

## FICTION

S ometimes it is simply more honest and effective to tell a story in a dramatized and fictionalized way so there is no need to tiptoe or skirt the issues. This is what I have done with the following story, *"Brass Poles."* I have done this for the sake of my reader—to give a true feel of what it is like to be a strip club bouncer. As a matter of fact, this entire book, *Stripped*, is actually derivative of a dramatic teleplay pilot I wrote about life at Cheetahs in Las Vegas—think, s*ex in the City meets The Sopranos in a Vegas strip club.*

When I am told that this story is too far-fetched to be believable, I can only smile. For those of us who were there, we know not only is the story not far-fetched, but rather typical. However, for everyone's sake—the guilty and innocent alike—remember, it is only fiction. Take it for what it is worth.

\* \* \* \*

# BRASS POLES

### A NOVEL

### (MORE OR LESS)

"I can't do this anymore."

"That's what you said last year."

"Yea, well, I was right last year."

"So, stay home."

One day I would. One day the clock would click over to 8:30 p.m., and I would just sit there. I would flick channels for a couple of hours and then I would go to bed with my wife, and I would wake up in the morning and get on with my life.

I pushed myself off the sofa, kissed Susan good night, and went to work.


"Sir, I question your commitment to heterosexuality," I said with my sweetest smile.

That did it. Pain exploded through my groin as my testicles were crushed against my pelvic bone. A fraction of an instant later, my nose was shattered, and a thumb was fish-hooking the inside of my cheek, tearing at the flesh.

This guy's really mad, I thought.

I tore his fish-hooking thumb from my cheek, and returned the favor of a broken nose with a snapping head butt of my own. He staggered backward, holding his gushing nose with both hands.

Amateur, I thought. I dug a straight right into his exposed stomach followed by a left to his liver. I would have doubled up the left hook, ripped one into his ear, but I was too slow and he was already falling out of my reach. Fucking Amateur.

My cheek hurt like hell. I kicked the little bastard in the ribs as he lay on the floor at my feet. My broken nose was pouring blood all over my shirt. I kicked him again. My balls. My aching balls. I kicked him again, twice.

Robert, the club's best bouncer, was standing by my side. "I think you got him bro," he said looking down on the man who was curled in a fetal position, gasping for air, and bleeding all over my boots.

"Look at my shirt," I said in my defense.

"Yea, that's messed up." Robert said.

We stood side by side looking down on the man.

"How much did he owe?" Robert guessed. He guessed right.

"A buck forty, but he doesn't have it."

"Mind if I try?" Robert asked.

"Be my guest. I'm going to go get cleaned up. See if they've got any extra shirts in the office."

"I'll have someone bring you one," Robert said as he knelt down next to the man on the floor. "You okay, buddy?"

I made my way to the men's room.

It wasn't pretty. I stripped off my ruined security staff shirt and dropped it on the floor of the men's room. Customers gave me a wide birth as they went about their business. I washed my face in the sink and looked into the mirror. My nose was broken, again. It was swelling already, but no worse looking than after the last time it had been broke. My eyes were turning black. The inside of my cheek hurt like hell. It felt like all the skin had been scraped out with the nasty side of a claw hammer. I checked my mouth in the mirror the best I could, opening wide and trying to get some light in there, but I didn't see any huge chunks of skin hanging loose, so I figured it would be okay. My balls hurt. They would for a week. I wanted to kick the guy again.

I looked in the mirror some more. There had been a lot of blood. I hoped the guy didn't have HIV.

Rick came in the men's room holding a new Brass Poles Staff shirt. He handed it to me with an accusing look. Rick was the club's general manager, and accusing looks were his speciality.

"Thanks," I said. I shook out the fresh folds and slipped it over my head, avoiding my still leaking nose as not to get it bloody. The shirt was too big for me. It needed to be washed, but at least it was clean.

"Well?" Rick asked.

I made myself busy tucking in the shirt and avoiding Rick's eyes as I answered. "The guy ran up a hundred and forty dollar lap dance tab on Shadow. He said he didn't have the money..."

"So you hit him?"

"He hit me," I corrected.

"Of course he did," Rick said. "Then you hit him."

"No," I corrected again, "then I defended myself to the best of my ability..." Rick joined in. We spoke in unison, "using the least amount of force to ensure my safety and the safety of the customers, employees and the suspect."

"But was all that really necessary?" Rick asked.

"Hey, I'm a titty bar bouncer. What do you think?"

"You're a gentlemen's lounge floor host," Rick said. "There are no bouncers any more."

"Oh yea, I forgot."

"Okay, okay," Rick said. "It goes in your report tonight."

"Yes sir."

"You okay?" Rick asked as an afterthought"

"Yea. Thank you for asking and caring."

Rick patted me on the back and left the restroom.

I shoved a couple pieces of wet paper towel up my nostrils and followed him out.

I struggled my way through the crowd to the VIP room where I had left Robert and the welshing customer. Robert was helping him use the ATM machine. Shadow, the entertainer who had been stiffed, was standing behind them, waiting. Robert would probably get the whole hundred forty dollars out of the guy, along with a thank you and a handshake. That's what made Robert the best, I thought.

I went back to work.


If there was one hard and fast rule here, and there weren't many, it was no pictures. The flash went off for the third time, and this time I was sure: it wasn't the strobe lights, it wasn't some moron flaming up an entire book of matches. It was a camera, and it was about to be mine.

I slipped through the crowd as quickly as I could, mindful of toppling drunks and spilling drinks, and snatched the camera from the young woman's hand. I might as well have slapped a banshee across the chops.

"What the fuck do you think you are doing you fucking asshole! Give me my fucking camera back you fucking prick! Where's fucking JB? I want fucking JB over here right fucking now! Give me my fucking camera you fucking asshole!"

I would have told her there were no cameras allowed in the club, but it was becoming painfully obvious that she already knew that, and she couldn't have cared less. What was also becoming evident was that fact that she didn't have to care.

I should have put the camera down then, mumbled some bullshit apology, and escaped the young woman as quickly as I could—asked for my balls back later. That's what I should have done, but there's something about pride that mutes your self-preservation instinct. Pride shushes that logical little voice in your head that is trying to tell you how to survive. Pride: she's a bitch.

"Why don't you just chill out a little. I'm not going to hurt your camera. I just want..." I tried to explain. I have no idea why I bothered.

"Fuck you! You know who I am? You know who I'm fucking? Do you?" She spat. She was like Eddie Griffin on crack with that mouth. "Jen!" She hailed the nearest cocktail waitress who was doing her best to pretend she was unaware of the situation. "Jen, tell this fucking asshole who I'm fucking!"

Jen sighed heavily and chewed on her bottom lip a little bit, as if weighing the decision whether to drop her tray and quit on the spot—face unemployment and potential homelessness—or to get involved. It was a toss-up. She made her decision and stood on her toes to whisper in my ear. Now it was my turn for a heavy sigh.

I finally did what I should have done in the first place. I placed the camera down on the table, and turned and walked away through the impossibly crowded club. Self preservation had finally overcome pride, and I swallowed my big mouthful of shit burger and went on my way.

You didn't mess with Joey's current bimbo-o-daweek. Now *that* was a hard and fast rule. Not if you wanted to keep coming to work. Not here.

Brass Poles was, if nothing else, Joey's club—his own personal bottomless ego well—and he ran it his way. That meant if some nineteen-year-old stoned-to-the-gills ex-stripper with an over inflated sense of self worth wanted to crawl up my ass with a handful of razor blades, some salt, and a lemon, so be it.

It hadn't always been like this. Back in the beginning, back when the owner still needed good people, you could count on his backing you—when you were right at least. Now the strip club was so popular, standing room only every night, and Joey was making so much money, good people doing their jobs were as disposable as Kleenex during allergy season here in Vegas.

I walked away through the shoulder-to-shoulder crowd, doing my best to block out the tirade that followed me, until the oppressive white noise of the club eclipsed even the screamed profanity of she offended. I didn't need her abuse. There would be plenty of opportunities for abuse on a Friday night at the Brass Poles Topless Lounge.

I have no idea whether they have cars in Somalia. If they do, I imagine they are not in very good shape—driven at break neck speeds with little regard for obstacles short of brick walls. I would also tend to believe pedestrians are in short supply in the impoverished country. I have formulated this opinion by witnessing the driving habits of the Vegas cabdrivers who drop customers in front of Brass Poles. I had to give them one thing though: They spoke more English than I spoke Somalian. But that was all I was giving them.

I had gone to the front door looking for a moment's reprieve from the thickly packed club, and had run directly into something infinitely more annoying.

"I drop five! Five guys!" The Somalian cab driver was emphatic to say the least.

"You dropped three. I counted them." Cookie, the doorman repeated—judging by the annoyed tone—for the tenth time.

"I drop five, five guys!" The Somalian was tiny in his size medium Izod shirt that draped on him like it hadn't been removed from the hanger. He looked malnutritioned even though he had probably been making five hundred-plus a night for the past year he had lived in the United States. Judging by the sweat that glistened on his face and his spastic mannerisms, he spent all his money on quadruple espressos to wash down his speed.

"Norm, you want to take care of this before I kill this little fucker?" Cookie asked me. So much for my moment of reprieve.

Even though the little shit cab driver probably didn't weigh a buck fifteen, a good two hundred pounds less than Cookie, I thought, in a fight, it might be a good match. Cookie was so bloated with steroids and insulin it seemed improbable he could even reach far enough around to wipe his own ass, much less kill anyone. He was already breathing hard, and all he was doing was standing there.

"Look," I said, speaking to the driver in a tone you would speak with a mutt dog—a retarded, piss-on-the-rug, useless, mangy, mutt dog. "If he says you dropped three, you dropped three. That's twenty-five bucks a head. Seventy-five dollars. That's pretty good, you should take it."

"I dropped five, five guys!" I was beginning to wonder if that was all the English he knew. The driver stood there looking up at me defiantly from chest height, his rotten teeth showing through his discolored lips.

The phrase "I drop five" was all any Vegas cabdriver really needed to know, and it was all our own fault. We had taught them everything they needed to efficiently steal from us. "I drop five." Five guys at twenty-five dollars bounty per head was an even one-hundred-twenty-five dollars. A buck and a quarter bribe for diverting customers from their intended destination, to Brass Poles. It was a common practice, all the strip clubs did it, we just did it better: we paid more. If you got in a cab and asked to go to the Crazy Horse, or the Olympic Garden, or Caesar's

Palace, for that matter, chances were you would end up at Brass Poles. Twenty-five dollars per head. We didn't ask how the customer got here so long as he did. Cabdrivers may well be crazy, but they are not stupid. Tack a couple of customers on to your total and see what it gets you? What's the worst that could happen?

I tried again to placate the driver, but in truth I didn't try very hard. I was confident of one thing at least: This little cab driving piece of shit wasn't my boss, or my boss' squeeze, and I was only going to tread so lightly. "You dropped three guys, you want the seventy-five or not?" I asked. Cookie handed me the cash the driver had already refused half a dozen times. I offered it to the little guy.

"Why you want to rip me off?" He asked.

So he did know more English. Something popped in my brain. A little something, but something. "Why you want to rip me off!" I shouted back at him. The driver took a step back. Crazy, not stupid. "Take the money and get the hell out of here before I shove it down your fucking throat." I crammed the money into his hand. The driver snatched it and started to move away. I knew he would turn. I just knew it.

"I never bring anyone here again!" The cabdriver shouted back at us when he was a relatively safe distance away.

I could have repeated the line along with him. I had heard it a million times. He would never bring anyone to Brass Poles ever again...until he had a car full of drunk tourists who didn't know any better, anyway.

Back inside, I thought, before something bigger popped in my mind and I introduced a cabdriver to Allah.

"Oh my god, you're giving me wood!" The grave-ly, booming, pro wrestler's voice carried even above the din of the packed dressing room. JB grabbed himself by the crotch as the girls squealed their amusement. "God, you shave the whole thing, you look like a twelve year old."

"JB, how would you know what a twelve year old pussy looks like?" Deanna wanted to know.

"I was in the Marine Corps in the Philippines back in eighty three...," JB began.

Deanna interrupted. "Okay, okay, I'll take your word for it. I don't need to know." She picked up a ciga-rette from the community pack on House Mom's desk and lit it with the disposable lighter that was chained to the desk with several links of rubber bands, like a low-budget bank pen.

The dressing room buzzed with activity as young women in various states of undress primped, preened, posed and bitched about the night. Deanna found an empty chair in front of a piece of dressing table that was littered with makeup, curling irons, and partially empty take-out food boxes. She plopped down in the folding chair, shoved some of the debris out of the way on the table, making enough room to put her feet up, and smoked her bummed cigarette.

Isis, a long slim entertainer with pale skin dotted with freckles, and petite breasts that would scoff at gravi-ty for many years, applied base makeup to cover a large tattoo on her shoulder. Deanna let smoke dribble from her lips and smiled up at Isis.

"How's your night, baby?" Deanna asked.

"I haven't been out there yet," Isis said in a tiny voice that was barely audible above the dressing room clamor.

"Well, you haven't missed anything," Deanna assured her. "The guys are cheap tonight."

Aubrey, a mousy entertainer with stringy hair and a bad complexion, took notice of Deanna's assessment of the night. Aubrey sat at the dressing table behind Deanna and played habitually with her limp hair. She eyed her best friend, Lori, who was applying liner to her lips. Aubrey knew Lori would get mad if she spoke with Deanna, but she liked her, nearly everyone did...except for Lori.

Aubrey tried to avoid Lori's quick, hard gaze as she spoke to Deanna. "If it's slow out there for you, it must really suck."

Lori answered before Deanna ever had the chance. "Yea, I'm sure she's really sucking out there tonight."

Deanna blew some smoke Lori's way and shot her a wickedly fake smile. "Bitch," she breathed, not quite under her breath.

"Whore," Lori retorted.

"Slut," Deanna shot back.

"Tramp!" Lori spat.

"Skank!" Deanna said turning fully in her chair and looking the other girl directly in the eye.

"Step up bitch!" Lori challenged.

Deanna never made a motion to stand. She simply smiled bigger as JB rushed across the room, his baritone voice nearly rattling the mirrors.

"Knock it off, both of you! I hate it when women fight...unless they're covered in chocolate syrup or something." JB's one track mind had nearly jumped the rail, but now it was back.

Lori was not ready to let it go. "That bitch started it!"

"Well I'm ending it!" JB bellowed. Deanna smiled sweetly. "Have you paid your tip out yet?" JB asked Lori accusingly.

"I already did." Lori's anger was quickly turning into a pout. "How come you always take her side?"

"I'm not taking anyone's side. Now get out there and get your ass to work." As JB spoke, his eyes and mind were already diverted by another young woman who stripped off her g-string unselfconsciously within full view of the manager.

Lori grabbed Aubrey by the arm and dragged her from the dressing room. Deanna shot her a saccharin smile as they left.

"Hey, Ice, you got any shows coming up?" JB asked Isis as soon as the young woman who had removed her g-string slipped on another.

"I'm between shows right now. I have an audition with 'Skin' on Thursday though," Isis said softly.

"That's the really dirty nude one downtown right?" JB asked.

"It's only topless, JB. It's a good show," Deanna said.

JB shrugged it off. The question had only been a set-up for his true interest in Isis anyway. "So you gonna let me do you once before you go off and be a big star in a show?"

Isis scoffed at the suggestion. "You know I don't do

men, JB."

"Oh Christ!" JB bellowed. "You just gave me wood!"

Deanna and Isis shared a laugh with half the dressing room. Isis pushed off the counter and headed for the door.

"At least you could let me watch," JB shouted after her.

Isis never turned around. She knew she would just be treated to an obscene picture of JB playing with his crotch and making lewd expressions.

Isis made her way down the long hallway from the dressing room to the club. The volume of the music and the hum of the crowd increased with every step. Isis hopped up the two steps into the DJ booth.

Dwayne, the hyped, coked to the gills, spastic, Brass Poles nighttime DJ, let out a machine-gun burst of barely coherent ramblings, as one song ended and the next began. "Come on boys, drop your cocks and put your hands together, a warm round of applause for Megan and Christy stepping down off the main stage. Don't forget to slip a tip on the hip 'cause it's hip to tip. Steppin' up next it's Brittany, dark hair, dark eyes, dark mind, three things that get me every time. Everybody say hooo...."

The crowd barely responded to the prompt, but Dwayne didn't seem to notice, or if he did, he didn't mind. He switched off the mic and rubbed frantically at his nose as if something had just flown up there and was making a nest. Isis waited for him to finish.

"I'm checking in. How long's the wait for stage," Isis asked.

Dwayne spun around like he had just been goosed by a ghost. "Hey Ice. I'll slip you in. About an hour, okay?" Isis might have responded, if there had been a pause. "Hey, you got another show yet? How's that going anyway? Hey, have I shown you a picture of my baby?" Isis was still shaking her head no to his first question as Dwayne snatched a wrinkled and smudged three-by-five photograph off the mixing board. "Here, check him out." He handed the photo to Isis. "He was seven weeks premature. Poor little guy's got some lung problems but he might get out of the hospital in another six weeks. I'm taking donations for baby stuff like toys and clothes for as soon as he gets out of the hospital, you know?"

Isis handed back the photo. "I just got here, I haven't made any money yet."

Dwayne took the photo and wedged into the gap under the mixing board. "That's okay, I'll talk to you later, okay?" Then into the microphone: "Okay boys, put those hands together for Brittany, second of two, time to drop the linen and start the grinnin'." Dwayne segued into the next song and Isis used the distraction to escape.


"Sir, you have to understand. You got the dances, you have to pay for the dances," I repeated testily. That's why I would never make a good father. I hated repeating myself.

"I never asked her for a dance," the customer stated smugly as if it made all the difference in the world. He was the type of guy who normally could talk to people that way and get away with it. A business man, or worse, a lawyer.

A professional type in his late forties with money and respect and power...in his own little world. Now he was in mine.

"Sir, I didn't ask you if you asked her for a dance. What I am telling you is this; you got the dances, you will pay for the dances."

I liked the word sir. I used it like a bigot would use a racial slur.

"We didn't have a contract. Nothing stated or implied. There's no signs, nothing stating what a dance costs or even what constitutes a dance."

I couldn't help but crack a small smile. A lawyer. I would actually enjoy this.

I hadn't made it ten feet back into the club after dealing with the cabdriver when a panicked entertainer had grabbed me by the arm and literally drug me to the table where I now leaned over the smug customer. She had been babbling something about doing three dances and the guy refusing to pay. I had gotten the gist of it. Same story a dozen times a night.

I leaned a little closer just to make sure the guy could smell the grilled salmon I had for dinner. "Sir, you can't tell me you didn't know you were getting a dance. When a naked twenty-year-old girl crawls onto your lap in a strip club, you've got to figure it's not because she finds you irresistible."

"Hey, I never asked," he said again, raising his palms up like he was helpless in the matter. Absolved of all debt.

This time I laughed out loud. "Now that's just igno-rant."

The customer took offense. "Are you calling me stupid?" He demanded to know.

"No sir. What I said was, you are ignorant." I wasn't laughing now. Now I was annoyed. "I could almost forgive stupid. Stupid people can't figure things out for themselves. You're smart enough, you're just ignorant thinking I give two shits about your opinion."

"Don't cuss at me," he said.

"Fuck you, you fucking fuck," I replied.

He seemed offended by my language. "I want to speak with the manager."

"No you don't," I assured him, "what you want to do is pay this girl."

"You don't know who you're talking to," the customer began. I put an index finger to his lips to silence him. He tried to push my finger away and I grabbed his face hard, pinching his cheeks together with one hand, so he looked like a gold fish sucking scum off the side of the bowl. "Hey, you can't do that," he said, or I think that's what he said. It was hard to tell with his face squeezed together like that.

"Can't or shouldn't?" I asked, happy to have a chance at my favorite line. "I think you are getting those two confused."

He tried to pull my hand from his face. Good luck. I could pinch together and carry two, flat, thirty five pound weight plates in the gym. He wasn't getting my hand off. Not without the skin coming with it.

Now it was my turn. "Sir. Just so you are not confused about who I am, or where you are, let me explain. This is not California. You are in Las Vegas. You are in a titty bar, and I am a bouncer. I am not a floor man, I'm not a host. I am a bouncer. What do you think is going to happen here if you don't pay this young lady what you owe her...sir?"

His eyes twitched to the entertainer who stood over my right shoulder, no doubt with a vindicated look on her face.

"Now, sir, you are going to pay this girl what you owe her. I'm not asking you, I'm not making a suggestion. I am telling you. Pull out your wallet, dig out sixty dollars, and do the right thing. You want to do this. Trust me, sir."

I let go of his face. He still had my finger prints on his cheeks. Sometimes that's enough. Usually blue-collar types get the message about then. They know you are telling them the truth. They work for a living. They would do the same thing in your position. Unfortunately, this guy was white collar all the way. He probably hadn't worked an honest day in his life, and the last time someone kicked the shit out of him he had run and told his daddy (lawyer senior) and they had addressed the matter at the next PTA meeting.

"Or what?" The customer managed though he didn't sound nearly as smug or confident now.

Or what, I repeated in my mind. By all rights I should have just grabbed him by the throat and pounded him in the face until my knuckles gave out. I should have began kicking him, and kept kicking him, until my shift was over or until the cops came to get me. A couple years ago I would have. There it was, proof: I was getting old. Or what. That was the problem with people today. There always had to be an alternative, an or what.

"Or nothing," I said. "You will pay her right now, or I will beat you, and then you will pay her, but you are going to pay her."

He looked up at me, his face flushed, his lips quivering. There was fear, but not enough. He didn't have any basis of reality to support his fear. This wasn't going to work. I was either going to have to do it: beat him and take his money; straight up strong arm robbery, or I was going to have to think of something else. I didn't want to use up my nightly beating quota in the first hour. I tired one last gamble.

"I'll tell you what. I'm feeling generous tonight. I'll give you an, or what. Here's what we are going to do. I am going to place you under citizens arrest and then I am going to call Metro. They are going to come down and write you a ticket for failure to pay for services rendered. It's pretty much the same charge as shoplifting, no big deal for someone like you. But then you are going to get a court date, and you are going to have to explain to our wife why you have to make another trip out here to Vegas. Then you can explain to some judge, probably someone in the owner's pocket, why after getting your dick rubbed for the better part of fifteen minutes by a girl young enough to be your daughter, you were too cheap to pay her what you owed her." The customer sat gaped-mouthed at the prospect. I kept pushing. "This, I've got to see. I'll be right there in the courtroom swearing on a stack of Bibles, I watched you get all three dances. It's worth sixty bucks to me just to see that." As the stunned customer watched, silent at last, I reached into my pocket and pulled out three twenties for the entertainer. She took the money, handed me back one twenty for my toke, thanked me, and left the two of us at the table.

It was a situation the customer could finally understand. That, or he knew full well I wasn't about to pay for his dances if I wasn't confident I would get my money back. Either way, he broke. Sixty dollars came out of a fat wallet that would never miss it.

"Thank you for doing the right thing sir. You'll sleep much better tonight," I said.

"Baby, I like the car, I really do," Deanna said. No one faked sincerity better than Deanna. "It was really sweet of you to get it for me, it was. But with the payments and the insurance and school and all...."

Her customer was heart broken to see Deanna in such distress. "Are you going to be short this month?"

"Don't worry about it," Deanna said as she diverted her soft brown eyes to the floor.

"I'm not worried about it. And you don't have to either," he said as he firmly turned her face to his.

Those eyes of hers, eyes that could make a fawn jealous, were moist with emotion. Deanna braved a smile.

A ridiculously thin, hunched shouldered cocktail waitress approached the table.

Deanna's customer, almost offhandedly from familiarity of repetition, signed the credit card receipt and took fourteen—of the fifteen—one hundred dollar bills from the waitresses tray.

"Thanks," the waitress mumbled before sulking away.

Deanna's customer just offered a brief nod of acknowledgment. He couldn't take his eyes off Deanna's. "How is school?" He asked.

"It's okay. I have this stupid sociology class. They make you buy like three books, one of them the teacher wrote herself."

"Expensive?"

"You wouldn't believe it," Deanna said.

"Yes I would. My daughter's in her second year at UCLA. You should have seen her credit card bill last month. I asked her how in the world can...."

Deanna's eyes were wandering the room. She was bored with the conversation.

"So, you feel like doing some dances?" He asked hopefully.

Deanna forced her attention back to her customer. "I'm not really in the mood," she said regretfully.

"Okay." Her customer's voice was heavy with disappointment. "I'll take a rain check."

The fourteen hundred dollars was pressed into Deanna's hand, and the customer received a peck on the cheek. "Baby, I've got to go freshen up. Wait right here," Deanna said as she stood.

Her customer was reluctant to let go of her hands. "You're coming back..."

Deanna just smiled and may have given a slight, vaguely ambiguous nod of her head.

As she walked away, he still could not take his eyes from her. Deanna was the most beautiful creature he had ever met, and he was in love. It was silly to think in those terms, he knew, but he couldn't help himself. She was so perfect, and the way she looked at him made him feel almost perfect too. When he was with Deanna there was nothing else in the world: no angry wife, no spoiled ungrateful kids, no lazy, incompetent employees. The world was perfect because it was just the two of them. The money meant nothing. Money was easy. You could always earn more money. There would be no other opportunity for a man like himself to be with a woman like Deanna. There was no price too high for that privilege.

Limos were almost as common as taxis in front of Brass Poles. Any Mope with a c-note, or group of ten with ten dollars each, could hire a limo and play big-shot for an hour. This limo was different: The group getting out of it could actually afford it.

Everyone recognized the kid as soon as he stepped out of the Stretch. Who wouldn't? His face had been plastered all over "Sports Center" ever since he had won the Heisman Trophy, and had been the first overall pick in the draft.

The obligatory entourage followed the star athlete from the limousine: five well dressed black men, laden with gold and brand names worn like badges of honor.

Another readily recognizable face, for those prone to watching a lot of MTV, posed for the crowd of onlookers before approaching the front door of the club.

The performing artist/personality, and unlikely choice for agent of the star athlete, sauntered up to Cookie and offered him a heavily ringed hand as if he were a dignitary expecting a kiss on the knuckles.

"Hey my man, I got...," the agent began.

Cookie interrupted. "Yea, I know who he is. First round pick right?"

"First pick over all," the agent corrected.

"Why don't you guys come on in. I'll let the manager know you're here." Cookie waved the entire group through the front door without bothering with trifles such as checking for proof of age, or the cover charge.


The com-line in the DJ booth buzzed incessantly. On the seventh ring, Dwayne answered.

"It's for you," Dwayne passed the phone to Rick who had been leaning in his regular spot in the DJ booth overlooking the club. Rick listened on the phone for a moment, then handed it back to Dwayne.

"You'll never guess who's here," Rick said, leaving Dwayne alone in the booth.

Dwayne didn't care who was here. As soon as the GM stepped out of the both, he quickly pulled a CD from its case, dumped some white powder from a tiny glass vile onto it, and began cutting up a line of coke on its shiny surface. Rick had been hanging out in the booth for nearly twenty minutes, and Dwayne was dying for his next bump.


"Hey, great to meet you guys," Rick gushed, pumping the star athlete's hand like a politician. "Man you gave me a scare in the bowl game last year. You almost cost me three grand on that one. How's that hamstring coming along anyway?"

"He's one hundred percent," the agent answered for his client.

"That's great, that's really great," Rick said, gripping the star athlete around the shoulders. "Can I get you guys a drink?"

"You got Cristal?" The agent asked.

"Not a problem. Hey Kevin!" Rick shouted to get the bouncer's attention.

Kevin lumbered through the crowd, shoving patrons roughly out of his way to get to the GM. Kevin's close set eyes, thick features, and the way he constantly craned his neck forward, made him look even less intelligent than he probably was.

"Kevin, see if you can get a table for five for these guys," Rick said.

"For five?" Kevin repeated, then headed back off into the crowd without waiting for confirmation.

Rick mumbled after him with disdain; "Yea, five. You know four plus one. Three plus two...genius." He turned to the star athlete's agent. "He'll let you know when he has a table for you. I'll go get your Champagne." Rick shook hands all the way around the group again before heading off for the liquor room.

"Hey boss, you wanted to see me?" I asked, poking my head into the liquor room.

"Yea, come on in here for a second. Close the door." Rick spoke without looking up. All his attention was on pouring the contents of a forty-dollar bottle of Monet Champagne into an empty three hundred fifty-dollar

Cristal bottle. "So what happened with Lisa Marie earlier?"

"Lisa Marie?"

"Skinny, blond, big tits, limited vocabulary...camera..." he added when he received no recognition from me.

"Oh yea. Someone was taking pictures, I grabbed the camera. I didn't know who she was."

"But you know now." His question was also a statement.

"I'm sorry. It's hard to keep up with who Joey's fucking. All I saw was a camera. I didn't stop to ask if she was blowing the owner," I said, but what I was thinking was, my mouth was going to get me into trouble one day.

"Yea, well, she says you twisted her arm when you took the camera. Says you called her some names, embarrassed her in front of her friends."

"I never touched her."

"Maybe you called her Joey's whore or something?" Rick had a troubling way of asking a question as if the answer were a foregone conclusion.

"Didn't say a word about it. Couldn't have called her Joey's whore. Didn't even know she was Joey's whore." Something about my mouth and trouble flashed through my mind again.

"Come on now...you didn't say anything to her?" Rick finished the bottle he was filling and looked up from his work. He laid the funnel aside.

"Not unless she could read my mind," I shrugged.

"Okay, okay, Joey's just gonna want to know. You know how he is."

"Yea, I know how he is," I said flatly.

I left Rick in the liquor room filling another empty bottle of Cristal, and wandered back into the fray on the floor.

I heard Kevin's angry voice chastising a customer over some trifle of a matter, but I didn't go to investigate. I wasn't in the mood. I knew how Joey was, everyone did.

Joseph Rizoli, the Brass Poles owner, had been born with a golden breast in his mouth. He was second generation. Raised to succeed his father in the multimillion dollar topless club business. Joey Jr. was a millionaire from the moment his daddy had given him his first club.

Joey's tirades were legendary. He would fire and rehire a single employee several times in a matter of minutes. He was like a child playing with dolls, shunning one, only to take it back into the fold until a whim took him again. Playing with lives and livelihood seemed to the only vice that still held interest for a man so jaded.

I nearly got one full breath. I walked outside looking for a reprieve from the smoke and noise, and I walked right into a maelstrom of shouting and insults in a language I didn't understand. Cookie was in yet another heated argument with yet another cab driver whose nationality I could only guess at. Cars and taxis were piled up in a mishmash of directions, clogging the thoroughfare in front of the club.

Tim, the indolent valet parking attendant, cell phone glued to his ear, was leaning in the window of a pimped out low-rider Beamer, talking to a somewhat androgynous-looking person with spiked blue hair.

Horns honked, cabbies cursed and I felt another permanent crease develop in my brow.

"Tim, Tim!" I shouted a second time. The valet's name might as well have been Tim Tim for all the good it did to call him once.

Tim looked over his shoulder at me, raising his eyebrows.

"Get this parking lot clear so we can see who the cabs are dropping."

Tim raised his chin at me and went back to talking to his friend. Tim made me very glad I didn't carry a gun.

"Tim! Hold your little car club some other time. Get this parking lot clear, now!" I shouted. Shouting at Tim always made me feel as if I had just shoved a sleeping cat off the arm of an easy chair.

Tim lethargically moved from the Beamer pimp-mobile and started waving is arms at cars and cabbies, giving them direction that even I couldn't decipher. I went back to see how Cookie was doing.

"Norm, I'm going to kill this guy if he doesn't get away from me," Cookie said, issuing his standard warning. "He dropped Samantha and Kim, and he wants me to pay him."

The cabdriver looked at me like he didn't understand. I tried to explain. "Those two girls you dropped off, they work here. We can't pay you for dropping off people who work here."

"My two were customers."

How did I know he was going to say that?

A harried cocktail waitress rushed to the front door in a panic. Her face was flush with excitement. "There's a fight out back!" She shouted.

I spun from the cabdriver and sprinted for the corner of the building. As I rounded the corner I heard heavy foot-falls and deep wheezing behind me. I turned to see Cookie, had started after me. His face was a deep shade of purple, and sweat popped out of his discolored skin.

"Stay at the front door," I shouted, and kept running.

Cookie stumbled to a stop, doubling over and wheezing heavily as he tried to regain his breath from the twenty-foot sprint. Customers gave the strange figure a wide birth as they passed him to enter the club.

I sprinted the length of the parking lot maintaining my breathing to make sure I wasn't gassed, just in case there was a fight at the end of the run.

I came around the back corner of the building and stopped dead. "Oh shit," was all I could think to say.

Kevin and JB were standing over the inert figure of a man who lay prostrate—face down—in a puddle of bar slop and puke, now reddened by the man's blood. The man's face looked like it had been run over a cheese grater.

JB was finishing applying a pair of handcuffs to the victim of the beating. Kevin was standing with all his three hundred pounds on the man's ankles.

I shoved Kevin off the man's legs. "What happened?" I asked.

"Fucker wouldn't pay Marissa for a dance. Wish you would have paid now, don't you muther fucker."

"JB, what happened?" I asked the manager, hoping for a more credible explanation.

"Hell, I don't know. I saw Kevin fighting with this

guy so I grabbed him," JB explained.

I knelt down next to the man and looked into his broken and bloodied face. His eyes were rolled back in his head, and his breath came in wet, gurgling spurts.

"Did you choke him?" I asked Kevin.

"Fuck yea. I choked the shit out of him. Fucker pissed his pants and everything."

I looked up at Kevin in disbelief. "This guy's going to need an ambulance," I said.

"Hell yea he is. I drilled him right in the mouth," JB proclaimed proudly.

"And call the police while you're at it. We're gonna need a cover story on this one," I said, looking back down on the brutalized face.

"All right," JB said. He stood from the victim, and headed for the back door of the club. "Make sure those pricks don't take my handcuffs this time." JB disappeared inside the club.

I looked back to Kevin. "How much did he owe her?"

"Twenty bucks," Kevin said, "but the guy was a real asshole."

"Okay, shit, let me think." Fuck, fuck, fuck, was the only thought coming to me. I looked at Kevin's thick, stupid, cruel features, and wanted to choke him to death then. I could have. I could have claimed the customer did it before we were able to come to his rescue. Fuck! My mind screamed. JB would never be able to keep it quiet. I would be caught. It would be worth it, almost, I thought.

"Okay, here's how it's going to go," I said, standing and looking Kevin straight in his thick-lidded eyes. "This guy sexually assaulted Marissa. He grabbed her by the crotch okay?" Kevin looked confused. I continued anyway. "Then, when you went to her assistance, he grabbed all her money from her g-string and tried to run. You attempted to stop him, and he hit you in the face."

"Shit," Kevin snorted, "that little fucker never got in a shot."

I truly wanted to kill him. "He hit you in the face," I reiterated more strongly this time. "He hit you in the face and you got dizzy. You were afraid for your life...."

"That little fucker couldn't do shit to me!" Kevin objected.

It was all I could take. I nearly lost my mind. "Look, you stupid piece of shit!" I screamed. Kevin shrunk backward away from me. "You beat this guy half to death over twenty dollars. If he's got any lawyer at all he's going to sue us for a million bucks. You want to go to prison? You want to get this club closed? You piece of fucking shit!"

"Hey, fuck you man. The guy deserved it," Kevin said defensively.

"Is that going to be your defense in court? Is it?" Kevin looked down and shuffled his feet. I already knew his answer. "Then do it my way and shut your fucking mouth."

"Okay. You don't have to talk to me like that," Kevin sulked.

"I don't want to talk to you at all, you fuck," I hissed.

Kevin looked at me with hate in his eyes, but he kept his mouth clamped shut. It was the only wise choice

I could ever remember him making.


"So, what else can I get you guys tonight?" Rick wanted to know.

There were several empty Cristal bottles, drained of their cheaper substitute, upside down in their slushy ice buckets. A girl was on every lap at the superstar athlete's table. The athlete's agent excused himself from the young lady on his lap and pulled Rick aside.

The two spoke in hushed tones and looked up to the main bar as they spoke. Rick nodded. His expression never changed at the request. The agent smiled, and Rick patted him on the back.

Rick put on his best host routine and spoke to the star athlete. "Why don't you come on up to the office. I've got a little something special for you." The star stood, and Rick put his arm around his broad shoulders. They headed toward the office. "Don't wait up boys," Rick said, winking back over his shoulder. The agent hurried after the two.

"What about me?" The athlete's agent looked stunned that he hadn't been invited for something special.

"Sure, why not?" Rick said, doing his best to conceal his revulsion. Something twitched in the corner of his eye. He smiled his biggest smile. "Plenty for everybody."

The three men made their way through the club.


Joey Rizoli stood watching the milling crowd from the steps leading to his office. It was another busy night. Every night was a busy night. Why not? He ran the best strip club in town. All you had to do was ask him. He would be more than happy to tell you. So what if every piece of upholstery on every couch and every chair in the joint was torn and frayed? So what if the carpet was so pocked marked with trampled chewing gum and cigarette burns that the original color was a mystery, even to those who had installed it? So what if the club got a couple dozen complaints a night from customers who could actually tell the difference between the premium drink they asked for (and paid eleven dollars for) and the generic watered-down swill they were served? He had taken home 22.2 million dollars last year, and that made him number one.

Joey watched his GM lead the two famous black men across the floor. He recognized the superstar athlete instantly, and grinned.

"Joey, this is..." Rick began to introduce the star athlete to the club owner. He was interrupted.

"Yea, I know who he is. He's on Sports Center every time I look up." Joey looked up at one of the muted televisions that played the sports channel in a constant loop, twenty four hours a day. Playing now was a story about women's soccer, but his point wasn't lost.

"Thought I'd show them a little Brass Poles hospitality," Rick smiled.

"That's cool," Joey said, "who you got?"

Rick stepped closer so he could whisper in Joey's ear. Joey almost laughed aloud, and nodded his head in understanding.

"I heard he was like that," Joey whispered. Rick just raised his eyebrows and cocked his head in acknowledgment. "Well, come on in. You guys have yourself a good time," Joey said, and stepped aside as he buzzed the security lock on the office door open.

Rick and his two new friends entered the office.

Joey stood on the steps and watched over his club some more with what might have been the closest thing he had ever known to pride.

Customers of every description, from Mexican construction workers, still in their work clothes, to Armani-suited conventioneers, milled and intermingled in the throng.

Young women of every shape, size, color, nationality...attached themselves to the customers with no prejudice as to their apparent station or lack thereof. Music, played at an intolerable volume, caused everyone—customers and entertainers alike—to shout over one another to be heard, creating a rumbling din of confusion as if the sky were continually falling around them.

"And I too am in Heaven," Joey thought.


Barry, the bar back who could have passed for Ricky Martin's little brother, approached Joey with a timid smile. He was thin, fine boned, and had perfect teeth, whitened by weekly bleaching.

"You need me in the office?" Barry asked Joey as he approached.

Joey just smiled and stood aside, allowing Barry to enter.

"I'm going to blow that one off," Deanna said. She couldn't play Dennis like she could her other sugar daddies. Dennis would never buy her a car or pay for her apartment or any of those other things her typical customers fought for the right to do. Dennis considered himself too savvy for any of that. Where Dennis used the word savvy, Deanna used the word cheap.

"Why would you blow that one off?" Dennis wanted to know. "That could be the break you've been waiting for. It's an audition for Baywatch Hawaii, who wouldn't want to do that?"

"Because I would have to go to Hawaii, and I don't fly. You know that," Deanna stated with the familiarity of speaking with a despised cousin.

"But it's Baywatch!" Dennis asserted. "Look what it did for all those other girls."

Deanna just shrugged as if the discussion were over. "I don't have anything to wear anyway. I'm just going to blow it off."

"What's to wear? It's a freekin' bikini for God's sake."

"You don't understand how Hollywood is. Just forget it."

"What if I take you shopping?" Dennis offered. "Would you think about going?"

"No," Deanna said flatly.

"Come on Dee, Forum Shops, a new bikini...."

Deanna cocked her head and smiled a tiny smile as if the offer was at least worth considering. "I would be gone for at least a month. I would lose my apartment, I would have to put my car in storage...."

"Deanna, don't try and play me." Dennis said with as close to anger as he could muster against the young woman.

Deanna was incensed. "I'm not playing you. You came in to see me. I didn't go to see you. You know what? Forget it. I don't even know why I talk to you about these things. You don't know anything about it, and you don't understand anyway." Deanna stood and tried to walk away. Dennis held her by the wrist. Deanna let him hold her.

"I'm sorry." Dennis pleaded. "Sorry, sorry, sorry..." That almost always worked when she was angry. "Look, Forum Shops tomorrow...anything...everything you want."

"I'll be too tired." Deanna said without looking down on the pleading customer.

"Well Sunday then."

"I'm going over to my sister's to play with my nieces on Sunday."

"Come on Dee, give me a break." Dennis was beginning to whine now.

Deanna sighed heavily—dramatically—giving in. "I'm having lunch at Spago's on Monday about three o'clock. If you want to be there, that's fine."

"I've got a client coming in on Monday..., " Dennis started to explain. Deanna tried to pull away.

"Whatever," Deanna said.

Dennis couldn't bring himself to let go of her wrist. "I'll finish with him early. I'll be there, I promise." Dennis said. He could tell Deanna was still angry. He couldn't even get her to look at him. She just stood there limp in his gentle grasp, staring off into the crowd. He had to get her to give in. He just couldn't stand it if she didn't. He wouldn't be able to sleep all weekend. He would call her, every hour. She wouldn't answer her phone. She wouldn't return his calls. He would be a wreck by Monday. He would be a mess with his client. He would be putting a three-quarter million dollar contract at risk all because he had fucked it up with Deanna. He knew all this from experience. With his free hand he reached into his pocket. "Order me a goat cheese pizza. I'll be there." Dennis deftly thumbed three, one hundred dollar bills off his roll, and offered them to Deanna. Deanna just turned her head further from him so she couldn't possibly see what he was offering. Dennis amended by thumbing off four more of the large bills. "If I'm late you can start shopping without me."

"You make me so mad sometimes," Deanna said, finally giving in and taking the money from his hand. She pecked Dennis on the cheek and favored him with a smile.

"Don't you want to do some dances?" Dennis asked.

"I'm not in the mood now," Deanna scoffed. "I'm going to go freshen up. I'll see you Monday," she said in way of dismissal. Deanna walked away through the crowd. Dennis could do nothing but watch her go.

The office was vastly understated and undersized. Four desks crowded the small rectangle, the largest of which split the room by a third, leaving what was left of the anemic space for the remaining three.

Joey sat behind the largest desk and fed papers through a steadily humming shredder over an already packed trash can. The star athlete's agent sat opposite Joey in a deep leather rocker. Rick sat perched behind him on the edge of another desk. Everyone else had already left the office. It was time to talk business.

"So you really think he's going to make those numbers this year?" Rick asked the agent.

"Did when I wrote up the contract," the agent said. "Now...shit. First the kid gets a lung infection or something, then says his hamstring is bothering him. Then during camp he gets this turf toe or some such shit. Always something wrong with him."

"Yea, that's a shame. Didn't get much up front huh?" Joey asked. A rhetorical question. Everyone knew what the star athlete had been signed for; the least up front money for a first overall pick in twenty years.

"Thought the boy could run for the gold," the agent admitted.

"I'm sure it will be fine," Joey assured him. "Either way, you're getting us those season tickets, right?"

"Absolutely," the agent agreed.

Joey gave Rick a look, and Rick went into the inner pocket of his sport coat and pulled out a fat envelope.

"Here's a little something for your trouble," Joey said as the envelope was laid on the desk in front of the agent.

The agent looked at the envelope. It was too thick with bills to close. He looked back up at Joey and smiled. Joey returned a smile that looked more like he had a bad case of gas.

"Look, just do us a favor," Joey said, "I hate to fly, so if your boy, or someone else on the team, say the quarterback, isn't feeling one hundred percent, give us a call and let us know, that way we don't have to fly all the way out there. You know, if the team isn't going to be playing that well anyway...."

The agent was staring down at the envelope as he answered. "Hey man, that's not a problem, you know?" He picked up the envelope and transferred it to his pants pocket.

"Great," Joey said, smiling genuinely this time. "Well, I'm sure you want to get back out there with your friends and enjoy the girls...or whatever."

The agent took the cue and stood. When someone handed you a fist-full of cash, you didn't sit around to see if they would want it back. "Yea, well I'll get you guys those tickets and I'll let you know..." He offered Joey his hand. Joey just leaned back in his chair and grinned up at the agent. Rick patted the agent on the back and shook his hand as he escorted him to the door.

"You guys have a good night now." Rick said, continuing the back-patting as he closed the door behind the agent.

Rick turned back to Joey and they shared a happy smile.

Joey shook his head in satisfied wonder. "Fucking Moolies."


So I perjured myself. That was nothing new. Every day it was something. Today would be no exception. I gave my report to the police. Kevin gave his version of my report to the police. The police took it without raising an eyebrow. Why not? It was easier than trying to figure out what really happened. Cops: the elevation of laziness and corruption to an art form.

Now this poor guy, handcuffed and bleeding in the back of the ambulance, would get his day in court. He would tell his story to his wife, then to the judge. Neither would believe him. He would plea the sexual assault and attempted robbery down to sexual battery. He would be released with three years probation, and have to go door to door in his own neighborhood informing his neighbors he had been convicted of being a sexual predator. His wife would leave him. His kids would try not to believe. Every day for the rest of his life he would wonder about the fatuous decision to argue with a steroid enhanced Neanderthal in a Vegas strip club over twenty dollars.

I looked to the East. The graying of the sky told me five a.m. was coming. It was almost over...for the night. Sometimes it felt like the night would never end. Like I was caught in an infinite time loop; a Rod Sterling nightmare. The Biblical Hell itself beneath our soles. But it did end—it always did—and the acts you had perpetrated were forgiven by your fevered mind, or at least buried deep beneath newer, fresher infractions. It was the clarity of every new morning that came with the rising of the sun, or at least the time marked by the merciless clock, that seemed to taunt its resistance to the five a.m. hour, that had me melancholy in my reflections. It was the fact that I had just finished writing an exceptionally creative incident report that colored the language of my thoughts.

The cops had all they needed, I still had another report to write. This one for the club's lawyers.

I wrote the lawyer's report and read it over, once.

That was all the attention it was going to get from me. It wasn't my best work, but it was after five a.m. now, and it would have to do. It didn't really matter anyway. A judge friendly to Rizoli would have the case assigned to his court, and the club's lawyers would have a easy time of it.

*At approximately three twenty a.m., I witnessed an entertainer (furthermore referred to as "Victim") being sexually assaulted by a customer (furthermore referred to as "Suspect"). The sexual assault consisted of Suspect forcibly grabbing the crotch area of Victim. I approached Suspect with the sole intent of halting the sexual assault when Suspect grabbed Victim's money from her g-string (approximately six hundred forty dollars) and attempted to flee the scene. I attempted to detain Suspect. Suspect then struck me in the face with his fist. I defended myself to the best of my ability, using the least amount of force necessary to insure my safety and the safety of the patrons and employees around me. The blows delivered by Suspect rendered me semiconscious, and I do not recall the details of the struggle that ensued. I was assisted in detaining Suspect by the shift manager. Suspect was handcuffed to prevent further injury to myself or Suspect. Las Vegas Metro Police were called, and Suspect was remanded to police custody.*

"Kevin." I shouted over the din of half a dozen different conversations that were taking place in the office at the same time: Bartenders, cocktail waitresses, bar backs, all counting money and bitching about their night. Kevin was in an animated rendition of his version of the incident to Robert and Big John, who exclaimed and laughed at all the right spots in his story. Kevin paused his story and approached where I sat behind the desk. "Read this report then sign it."

Kevin read the report, moving his lips only slightly as he sounded out the bigger words. I watched his face wrinkle in repugnance as he read the part about having been hit and knocked semiconscious. Let him screw it up in court, I thought. I couldn't care less at this point. I just wanted to get home and get in bed. The club could burn to the ground for all I cared, as long as I was home in bed when it happened.

I closed the front door behind me, easing it shut as not to wake Susan. I stopped at the kitchen, poured myself a bowl of cereal and doused it in milk, before heading to the living room.

The sweat and smoke-drenched shirt came off and went on the floor along with my discarded boots. The bowl of cereal balanced on my stomach as I switched on the television with the remote.

CNBC was already running their stock tickers for the pre-market trading. I spooned large heaps of the gawd-awful sugary-sweet cereal into my mouth, and watched the symbols go by. Qualcom's ticker passed: sixty seven and change. I wouldn't be retiring anytime real soon. I switched off the television.

The soft clicking of claws on the kitchen tile floor announced the arrival of my sleepy-eyed dog. Kiko padded her way across the living room carpet to sheepishly greet me, as if feeling guilty for having taken so long. The apologetic lay of her ears and the coy wag of her tail let me know she was glad to see me, even if I had awaken her from her sleep. Or maybe it was just the unfinished bowl of cereal that she was happy to see. I wasn't taking any chances. There were few enough who were glad to see me under any circumstances. I wasn't going to put this one to the test. The unfinished cereal bowl went on the floor for the little beggar. I went upstairs.

Susan was in bed, or I assumed it was Susan under the huge mound of covers that left my side of the bed barren, but for a thin sheet. I shucked the rest of my clothes and eased onto the bed.

I was grimy with sweat and saturated with smoke, but I was also beyond exhausted. Besides, I always felt awkward about showering after work.

In the beginning of our relationship, Susan and I would jump into bed about six seconds after I hit the front door. We couldn't keep our hands off each other. But that was fifteen years ago, and it had been two o'clock when we had been coming through the door, not six.

Susan wasn't waking up. I wouldn't have been able to do her much good if she had.

I didn't shower because I didn't want to give my wife one more thing to worry about. It was bad enough I was working around a couple hundred beautiful twenty-year-old women until all hours of the morning. Jumping in the shower the second I got home seemed...well, suspicious. Maybe I was just lazy.

"Good morning baby. How was your night?" Susan's sleep-husky voice was muffled from behind the wall of covers.

"I haven't counted it yet." I lay down and covered myself with a corner of sheet, and stared up into the darkness.

The last thing I remember was the soft snoring coming from the mound of blankets beside me.

"They beat the living hell out of that guy."

"I've seen worse."

"Yea."

"I'm sure I have. I just can't remember when."

"Rodney King."

"Shit, I'd of shot that big fucker."

"This sucks. You want to pack it in. Sun's up. Everyone's gone for the night anyway."

"We need someone on the inside."

"So, request undercover."

"Fuck that. I'm married. My wife freaks just knowing I'm sitting across the street from a titty bar all night."

"So, your wife running this operation now?"

"Fuck you. Why don't you request undercover?"

"I did."

"What'd he say?"

"He said, if I could find a way in, knock myself out."

"Your chest gets any bigger, and you can go in as a stripper."

"Fuck you, I'm natural."

"Yea, right, and I shave this bald spot in the middle of my head. So go in as a bouncer."

"I could. Those guys ain't that big."

"A couple of them are."

"Not the bald one, or the Mexican one."

"So?"

"So what? Bouncers don't know shit. If someone goes in, they got to be in deep, close to Rizoli."

"Like who?"

"Like, how the hell should I know? If I knew that, I'd be running this operation. I wouldn't be sitting out here sweating my balls off in this tin can with you. I'd be in there in the air conditioning getting blown all night."

"I thought you loved me."

"Yea, well, I love air conditioning and getting blown more. You got time to stop off for a beer before you go home?"

"Yea, I told my wife I was working 12 on and 12 off, so I got about three hours before she starts freaking out."

"Aah, honesty; the foundation of all lasting relationships."

"How many times you been married again?"

"That's not because I wasn't honest. It's because I got caught."

"Hand me the keys. So, the bar at the Rio?"

"The Palms' got better looking hookers."

"Palms it is."


I woke up the same way I always do, with a dull panicked feeling that the phone was ringing. I had a caffeine and second-hand smoke hangover. My throat was sore and clogged with mucus. My nose was sore and clogged with dried blood. The inside of my cheek was killing me. I didn't even want to think about my balls. My eyes burned when I opened them.

The digital alarm clock by my bed said it was 10:37. Perfect. I had gotten my full four and a half hours of sleep. It was the same four and a half hours I had been getting for the past six years since I had switched from days, to the graveyard shift. My body had never really adjusted.

The bedroom was pitch black from the several layers of heavy curtains Susan had sewn herself to cover the windows. The house was silent. Still, like clockwork; 10:30 every day I came awake anticipating the phone call.

I rubbed my burning eyes and tried to swallow. My throat hurt. Shouting above the din of the club and sucking down second-hand cigarette smoke wasn't doing my voice any favors.

I swung my legs over the side of the bed and pushed myself to a sitting position. The standard rush of vertigo spun up through my head, then slowly dissipated. I rolled my neck to the right, got three good cracks, then to the left and got two more. I arched my back and rolled my shoulders, but apparently, that was all the cracking I had in me. I circled my feet and listened to my ankles do their imitation of a bowl of Rice Krispies. My feet felt like they were treading over sharp, hot glass, and I hadn't even stood up yet. No sense putting it off. I took a deep breath and stood. Now my feet really let me now about it. The sense of vertigo returned as I stood, and I braced myself against the bed with one hand until it passed.

I hobbled to the bathroom like a rodeo cowboy who had gotten the wrong end of an eight second ride on a Brahma bull.

I emptied my bladder and limped to the shower without acknowledging the mirror above the sink. I wasn't anywhere near ready for what it had to say this morning.

I stayed in the shower until the guilt of the capricious amounts of water I was wasting compelled me to get out. I dried off, and finally looked into the mirror.

"Jesus Christ." The lines around my bloodshot eyes seemed deeper, my skin was blotchy red form the steaming hot shower, and the Basal-cell skin cancer above my right temple looked angry and in need of another dose of liquid nitrogen. Both my eyes had deep black lines beneath them. My nose was swollen about twice it's normal size. Susan would be thrilled.

I opened and clenched my fists a few times. The arthritis didn't seem to be getting any worse, so I had that going for me.

The asshole who said pain was your body's way of letting you know you were still alive, didn't mean this kind of pain. He meant the clean, crisp, life-affirming pain of being slugged in the teeth. Not this dingy, rotting throbbing, aching bullshit. This was the sort of pain only death could relieve.

People talk about creaky knees, but until you feel them creak, I mean, actually creak, you have no idea how accurate that word truly is. I made my way down the stairs, gently, one at a time.

Susan was on the couch with her legs curled up under her, a blanket wrapped around her feet in difference to the air conditioning, though it was probably already 104 degrees outside. She was browsing the internet on her iBook computer, eliminating numbers from the morning paper's sudoku puzzle, and watching a documentary on ancient Egypt, on TV: Women and their multitasking. I could barely remember where we kept the coffee mugs.

"Good morning baby, you did good last night," Susan chirped, before she looked up.

I grunted in response.

There was a neat row of cash piled up on the kitchen counter reserved for mail and money. A small stack of hundreds, a tall stack of twenties, and two stacks each of fives and singles. No fifties. No one in Vegas used them. They were bad luck. It looked like a decent night.

Kiko wagged her way toward me and greeted me with a sniffing of my empty hands, just in case I had some-how become considerate enough to remember to bring her a doggie treat. She generously settled for a good ear rub-bing.

Susan finally looked up and saw what was left of my face. She got that look she always got and put down what she was doing. She stood and went to the downstairs bathroom and came out with a blue ice bag. She filled it from the ice dispenser in the freezer door and set it on the counter beside the coffee maker. She let her hand drag across my shoulders like I was a horse about to be put down. She went back to the couch without saying a word.

God, I loved that woman.

I finally remembered where we kept the coffee mugs. Not that they had moved for the year we had lived in the house. I filled the biggest one I could find with cold coffee from yesterday's pot. I put the mug in the microwave, set it to scalding, and began looking for the aspirin.

"I've got to go to the store today. You need anything?" Susan asked.

"Not that I can think of," I said, but I probably couldn't be called on to remember my middle name at the moment.

Susan laid aside her several projects and got off the couch. She was already dressed in a cute little flower print sun dress. The one where the top two buttons always came undone under the pressure of deep breathing. "I'll have my cell phone if you think of anything."

I nodded.

She came over to where I was standing in front of the microwave, watching my coffee go round and round, and kissed me on the back of the neck. I felt the same shivers I had for the past thirteen years when she kissed me there. She left.

She always told me to call her if I thought of anything I needed. I had never called. Susan had never once left me wanting for anything.

I stopped the microwave and took my coffee out just after it began boiling. I shuffled to my favorite chair in the living room with Kiko on my heels. By the time I had finished my coffee, scanned the news paper, and learned about agricultural methods of ancient Egypt, it was coming up on noon, and I was ready to start my day.

My knees wouldn't take jogging, so I walked up to the park and used the 30 yard grass covered embankment to run sprints. Running up hill delivered less pounding to the knees. Your foot didn't have to fall as far to reach the ground on a steep incline. I preferred sprints to distance running anyway. A good fight lasted about the same amount of time as a 30 yard sprint. That, and I figured if anyone could outrun me over that distance, they deserved to get away.

Mothers who brought their children to the park, and sat in the shade of the gazebo while their children played on the plastic jungle-gym sets, watched me with lust. At least that's how I imagined they were watching me. Their looks may have just been wonder at who could possibly be stupid enough to run sprints up a hill in 112 degree weather.

I liked being able to do what other men couldn't do. What they weren't willing to do. Besides, it was a dry 112.

Susan was already home by the time I returned from the park. She was on the couch, on the internet, doing presumably another sudoku puzzle, and watching a documentary about the Winchester mansion on A&E.

I went out into the garage and lifted some weights.

My neighbor thought I was crazy, and told me so every time he saw me lifting weights or hitting the heavy bag in my garage. Garages in Vegas, during the summer, generally could double as sauna's. He spent about the same amount of time in his garage, polishing his car, or dinking around with his speed boat, as I did working out, so that made us even. I thought he was crazy too.

Apparently the shopping Susan had done was grocery. The refrigerator was packed to bursting with milk and meats and cheese and salad fixings. I made myself a protein shake. I was too tired to eat a proper meal, and I needed to get a nap before I headed down to jiu jitsu practice to get tied into knots by men half my size and half my age. Susan would have a solid meal ready for me when I got back. Then I could shower and get ready for work. My day would be complete.

"All right, first an announcement. We got the funding for a deep cover op. We're going to need some names."

"Not one of us?"

"No. Not on this one. Too much potential for cross contamination. We need to be tight. I need some names. Who do we have?"

"I've got a Armando Salazar. We got him on transporting with intent."

"Coke?"

"Yea."

"Rizoli's not into coke. Besides Salazar's, what, Mexican...?"

"Salvadoran."

"Whatever. Remember, this Rizoli's a racist as they come. We need a white man, preferably Italian."

"Dale Wolfson; hijacking and interstate fraud. The guy's covered in Neo-Nazi ink."

"There's a possible. Have you used him before?"

"Once."

"And?"

"Didn't work out. We put him in with the Mongols. It took the bros about ten minutes to figure out he wasn't one of them."

"The guy sounds like a rock."

"Yea, well, what do you want?"

"Someone who's not a rock...come on people. We've got to have someone."

"Tony Cambina; Steroids and pharmacuticals. He says he worked with the Greek families out of New Jersey as an enforccr."

"Cambina? That doesn't sound Greek?"

"He's Italian, I think. He looks Italian. His last name ends in a vowel."

"You use him before?"

"Twice. The first time, when we originally busted him, he gave us every connection in his pharmacutical chain from Mexico to Michigan. Steroids mostly. And once on a murder-for-hire sting."

"And?"

"Convictions on everything. We got the idea for the murder for hire because he told us he took a hit for 20 grand once."

"He confessed to murder?"

"No. He said he kept the money and backed out of the hit because the client was, and I quote, 'a dumb shit and didn't have anyone to complain to.'"

"Can he get away with wearing a wire?"

"He could get away with wearing a rccl to reel. The guy's a big as a Rhino. All he ever wears are those Golds Gym shirts. You know, those tents that make you look twice as big as you are. He's probably got seven of them, one for each day of the week. He's six foot one, three hundred fifteen pounds."

"Jesus Christ. Sample his own wares?"

"Big time."

"What's he looking at?"

"The original sentence was 12 to 20, so he's pretty much into us for life."

"All right. Sounds like we've found ourselves a winner. Talk to him. Scare him first. Tell him he'll do the whole twenty if he screws this up. Tell him what it pays, and what we need. Give him something that will get him in tight with Rizoli, then let him go. But keep a leash on him. I don't want one of those Atlanta fiasco's. This could be a precedent setter, people. We need to stay looking rosy on this one. All right, that's it. Everyone else keep doing what you've been doing, and keep me up to date."

Being punched in the face will get your attention. This guy got all of mine. He had a good punch; my ear was still ringing and felt swollen, numb and tingling all at the same time. His second punch didn't do much but add to the black eye I already had. The left one. His third punch completely missed. Fucking amateur.

Robert had his guy in a Muay Thai clench and was dropping knees into his gut with perfect rhythm that made it look as if they were dancing.

Big John had his guy by the throat, up against the wall, and had already begun on one of his famous profane, ranting lectures.

My guy was out cold from a rear naked choke. My second guy was the one who had just rung my bell.

Cookie and Kevin were nowhere to be found, as usual.

I normally wouldn't hit a guy in the face, but I was

a little embarrassed at getting tagged, right out there in front of customers, cab drivers, God, and everyone else, so I made an exception.

The guy was bouncing around like an epileptic Muhammad Ali. I blitzed him; my feet continually shuffling me forward, my punches coming short and straight from my shoulders. Heedless of anything he might throw back, I just kept punching. I could keep that up for about twenty seconds on the heavy bag. It only took three and a half. He turned his face away and crumbled to the ground in a fetal position with his head wrapped in his arms. Fucking amateur.

I kicked him twice in the ribs while he lay there just to make sure there were no thoughts of getting back up. His friends shouted their protest of my tactics. They had to shout. They were already half way across the street when the fists started flying

There were three more guys in the bachelor party, but they didn't seem to want any of what their friends were getting—conscientious objectors, no doubt—and they watched from a safe distance away as their friends were brutalized.

Four out of the seven had fought. That was better than average. Normally, one guy went down, and the rest of the party suddenly developed a moral conscience against violence.

Robert's guy was huddled on the ground crying—actually crying. Big John's guy was turning all sorts of unnatural colors from the prolonged lack of oxygen.

Neither of my guys were moving much at all.

"Big John, I think you got him," I said, approaching

the two and looking closely at the victim of Big John's wrath.

"Fucking little punk bitch..." John spat his tirade in a continual stream of profanity. His face was nearly the same color as his victim's. Thick purple veins protruded from his temples—Big John's—and sweat streamed from his tight crew cut, down his contorted face. I was pretty sure the guy in Big John's grip would pass out pretty soon if I couldn't get him to loosen his grip, but I was positive Big John would have a coronary. These 'roid rages were no good for his high blood pressure.

"What do you think Johnny? You wanna go back inside and make some money?"

That got his attention. At least he was thinking of something other than crushing a throat now.

Big John tossed the man side like a rag doll. He smiled at me. "Bro, I got this guy in the VIP room. He's tokin' me like a C-note every time he comes back from taking a piss."

"How's his bladder?"

"I'm buying him Corona's. Those things make you piss like a race horse."

"Who's he with?"

"Lacy. He'll be back there all night."

By now, Big John was eager to quit talking to me and get back to the VIP room, and his hundred-dollar customer.

Robert was already at the front door checking ID's and taking cover charges in Cookie's absence.

I would have to find Cookie and let him know the fight was over and it was safe to return to his spot at the front door.

The beaten bachelor party was making their way across the parking lot toward the taxi line, shouting back at us how they would come back and kick our collective asses. I went looking for Cookie.


I envied, and felt sorry for the guy all at the same time.

Deanna was straddling a customer I had never seen her with before. That was rare for Deanna. She normally stuck with a extremely select group of regulars. As a matter of fact, I had never seen her approach a customer, cold, in the club as long as I'd known her. Her customers always came in with a single-minded purpose: to see Deanna. I don't know where she recruited them, if not the club, but she never seemed to be lacking for attention, so whatever she was doing, it was working.

She held the customer's face in both her hands and looked into his eyes.

She had looked at me like that—once—before she realized exactly how married I was. It was a scarry look. It was a look that made you understand why men went to war. Now she looked at me differently, and that look was even worse.

She ran her long nailed fingers through the man's hundred dollar hair cut, past his gray temples, down his neck. Her lips were moving. I couldn't hear what she was saying from where I was standing, but I was mesmerized by the motion of her lips. I was lost. As lost as the customer. I couldn't see his face. His back was to me, but I knew what he was feeling just the same.

Deanna gently and slowly, pressed the man's face between her breasts and cradled him there. She looked up into my eyes.

I swallowed hard.

Deanna let her eyes trail from mine and turned back to her customer. She pushed his head back against the chair. She leaned to him. Her lips brushed his ear.

"I need to...um, I need to go to the ATM," the customer stammered.

"Take your time baby, I'm not going anywhere," Deanna said. She slid off the customer's lap and elegantly reclined in her own chair.

The customer self-consciously adjusted himself and stood. Deanna watched the customer until he disappeared into the crowd. She smiled at me and stood.

Watching Deanna stand was like watching a priceless pearl necklace being drawn from...well, I don't know what. Something thick and viscous and molten and priceless. The human language isn't adequate. At least not my vocabulary.

She made her way to where I stood, slid her hands up my stomach to my chest then around my neck. She pulled my head forward and kissed me gently on the swelling beneath my black eye. It made me wish my other eye had been dotted also. In her eight-inch platform heels, she was just tall enough to do that. I kept my hands at my sides. I didn't dare touch her. I couldn't. She didn't expect me to. It was just our version of a handshake or a high-five. Sometimes it was very good to be me.

"What's the other guy look like?" Deanna asked,

checking the bruises on my face.

"Worse than me," I admitted.

"You really should learn a different fighting technique."

"Technique?"

"I mean, other than waiting until he's broken both his hands on your face before you start fighting back."

I grimaced in memory.

One night, a couple years ago, the fighter who had ended my brief, but inglorious kickboxing career had come into the club. Deanna had been his choice for company that night. The fighter had gone on to glory as a champion UFC fighter. He had told Deanna how he had broken his right hand on my face, and how I had kept coming at him. She told me he had spoken with respect. I knew it was wonder. Wonder at how anyone could be stupid enough to take such a beating and not have the brains to lay down. That was my kickboxing claim to fame: I'd had the living shit kicked out of me by the best fighter in the world.

"How's your beautiful wife?" Deanna asked.

"She'll be a whole bunch better when I get home tonight," I said.

Deanna giggled. It was a rich sound; evil, almost. "Glad I could help."

"Did I hear your customer say he was going to the ATM?"

Deanna swayed back and forth gently against me. She never really stopped moving. I'll bet there were ripples moving through her body when she slept. I tried not to dwell on the thought. It made me sweat. Her breasts brushed my stomach. I flexed my abs.

"He's new. He doesn't know any better. After that three hundred, I'll give him an education about credit card cash advances."

"There's no better teacher."

She purred. Humans aren't supposed to be able to do that. Deanna can. She put her hands on my stomach to acknowledge what she had felt with her breasts. "Lift up your shirt."

"Shit," I said.

"Just a little," she giggled again, pulling gently at my shirt.

I tried to move away. I didn't try very hard. "I'll give Susan your love," I said.

"When are you going to let me give her my love?" Deanna asked.

I couldn't take it. "I've got to get back to work. You too," I said. Her customer was returning.

She gently tucked my shirt back into my pants and kissed me on the side of the mouth. "Walk me out tonight."

I nodded and forced myself to walk away from her. Looking at Deanna was like looking into the sun. Even when you looked away, the image was still burned there. It was worse when you closed your eyes. I was afraid to close my eyes around Deanna. I needed to keep my eyes wide open and remain aware at all times. Deanna scared the shit out of me.


"What the fuck's that stupid whore want now?" Joey sat behind his desk feeding his paper shredder. There was no venom in the question. It was simply a question.

"Nothing really," Rick said. "Her son and some friends are coming in later. She wants to see if you can take care of them."

Joey looked up from his shredding. "What, like get him laid?"

"I was thinking more like a couple of beers and some lap dances," Rick said, then paused thinking; had she meant the other?

Rick sat opposite Joey, across the desk in the office. He was thumbing through a porn magazine, waiting for Joey to finish what he was doing so they could go get some dinner.

A very pretty, very nervous looking man, Terry, quietly lied to his wife on his cell phone in the far corner of the office where Joey and Rick couldn't hear and make fun of him.

"Whatever. Go ahead, take care of it," Joey said. "No more than five hundred in dances though. The bitch is already into me for 15 grand for her daughter's ski school, and I put that down payment on that fucking truck for her and she hasn't even voted on the measure yet." He was really beginning to hate the city council.

Terry said good-by to his wife and joined the conversation; "She's voting yes."

Joey and Rick continued to ignore Terry, as they usually did.

"It hasn't even come up in front of the city council yet," Rick said.

"I know it hasn't come up in front of the council yet. Jesus Christ, I'm sitting on three million dollars worth of construction loans. You don't think I know it hasn't come up in front of the council yet? You dumb fuck."

Rick laughed a little. "Okay, okay, geeze. I can see someone needs a nap."

Joey grinned without looking up from his shredding.

Terry laughed a little to show he was in on the joke.

Rick looked over the edge of the magazine he was flipping through, recognized the grin on Joey's face, and decided to run with it. "City council meeting's on the 12th. We've got both Mikes, Kerry, Sanchez, and Ms. Anderson will be right there for us. As long as we take care of her son, and your fat ass doesn't have a heart attack before the vote, it's a slam dunk."

"It's a slam dunk," Terry said.

"Fat ass, shit. What's your ass weighing now, about 250?"

"Shit, I was 245 coming out of college."

"Yea, well, I'm only two and a quarter, fat ass."

"Yea, but you're about, what, five four?"

"Fuck you. Don't forget who pays your bills, boy."

"I'm just sayin', looking down on the top of your head all the time's got me thinking; Maybe I should invest in Rogaine stock."

Joey laughed and missed the shredder completely with a stack of papers. "Fuck you, you bald, hair-plug wearing fuck. You look like one of my kids fucking dolls."

"All right, all right, I didn't mean to make you defensive. I know how testy you get when you haven't eaten. Let's go get some dinner."

Terry fidgeted uncomfortably in the corner. It had

always been that way, ever since high school. Joey and Rick, tight, everyone else on the fringes. Terry had gone on to be a cop, and then got elected to a term on the city council, but he still couldn't get Joey's respect. Now Joey called him his bag man. He hated that. Terry preferred the term, lobbyist.

Joey turned off the shredder.

"You want to run down to *Nine*?" Rick suggested hopefully.

"We'll go anywhere you want. You're buying." Joey said.

"Appleby's it is," Rick amended, and followed Joey out the back door of the office.

Terry hurried through before the door closed on him.

It had been the same way since he had met Joey in tenth grade, Rick reflected: Joey and his tirades, Rick and his easy-going acceptance of the abuse. Joey didn't mean anything by it, Rick knew. It wasn't Joey's fault. What did you expect when you grew up the son of a multimillionaire strip club mogul? Nothing had ever been off limits to Joey. He had been able to say and do whatever he wanted all his life. He had an entire crew of sycophants, like Terry, following him around like he was some sort of rock star or something. Rick had been the only one in high school to ever stand up to Joey. He knew that was probably why they had become such good friends. He was the only one of his friends Joey respected.

Of course, it had been easy for Rick to stand up to Joey and his bull shit. Rick had been on his way to the big leagues. Heavy recruitment from high school to college.

From college to the minors. A 245 pound, six foot six White man with a thunderbolt for a right arm: Ninety-three-mile-per-hour fast balls, wicked breaking stuff...as solid and consistent as they came.

Rick's god-given gifts had gotten him to the Bigs. Problem was, everyone in the Bigs was blessed: Everyone was big and sturdy and had wicked breaking balls and 90-plus mile-per-hour fast balls. Everyone had thunderbolts for arms. The difference between those who stayed, and those who went, wasn't physical. It was mental. Rick hadn't discovered that until he was back on the block working as a strip club manager for his abusive, prick, son-of-a-bitch high school buddy.

Still, a quarter mill a year for all the twenty-year-old ass you could shake your stick at, wasn't so bad.

"Sir, how much do you owe her?"

"I already paid her fifty."

"Sir, I didn't ask how much you paid her. I asked how much you owe her." The question seemed to be going over his head. I tried to simplify it for him. Sir, dances are twenty dollars per song. How many dances did you get?"

"He got eight," the curvaceous young woman stated from behind me. Her accent was something exotic. I held my finger up to silence her, without looking back. I wanted to hear more of that voice, but didn't need an argument between the two. I was going to give the customer enough rope to hang himself with. The young woman was silent. I had never collected for her before. She showed promise.

"I didn't get no eight dances," the young man said without conviction.

"He didn't get no eight dances," one of the customer's friends parroted.

The customers were young—early twenties—and had the look of college students; the soft, hind-tit fed look of having been spared the real world their entire lives. There were three of them at the table. This would be good for them, I thought.

A ridiculously cute, plump entertainer sat on the lap of the parrot customer and nearly inperceively nodded her head, "yes," confirming what I already assumed: The young man had completely lost track of how many dances he had been getting. A person couldn't hardly blame him, I thought. If I had that curvaceous, exotic voiced woman sitting on my lap, half naked, I wouldn't have been able to count to eight either. Still....

The third young customer sat slumped in his chair, alone, and looked resigned. He looked like he knew how this would ultimately turn out. I wondered if he had met me before, in a similar circumstance.

"So, how many dances would you say you got?" I asked the young man.

He shrugged, "Five or six, maybe."

"So, maybe six," I confirmed.

"If that," the parrot added.

"And you paid her fifty dollars, right?" It was fun to watch a drunk college kid try and do math in his head, even simple math. "So, even by your own count, you still owe her seventy dollars, right?" That was me, Uncle Norm, trying to help out.

The young man chewed on his lip a little. "I probably got like two or three dances," he said.

I laughed and smiled at his two friends.

Robert had appeared behind the parrot customer. Even though Robert never wore his Brass Poles Security name-badge, there was no mistaking him for anything but a bouncer. He just had that presence.

I didn't look around for any more security. We wouldn't need any, even it this turned ugly.

"Now, son, that's just silly," I said. "She says eight dances. You said six. Let's compromise. Pay her for seven. That's another ninety dollars. No big deal, right?"

The quiet, resigned customer was already reaching for his wallet.

The three pooled their money and came up with eighty seven dollars and sixty cents. I let them keep the sixty cents.

By the time I had collected the money and handed it over to the entertainer, Robert had already disappeared back into the crowd. The guy moved like a ghost. I wished I could move through a crowd like that.

"I'm sorry," Miss Curvy said when I handed her the eighty seven dollars. She deftly checked the total and handed me back twenty seven. "I shouldn't have run a tab." Her accent was Brazilian, maybe. "What happened to your eye?"

"The last guy didn't have the eighty bucks," I explained.

"I'm sorry. I won't do that again," she said, and actually looked sorry.

"Sure you will. But that's okay. It's why I get the

big bucks. What's your name?"

"Arianna," Miss Curvy said. She didn't ask mine. She patted me on the hand and went back to work. I watched her go. It was a wonderful thing to watch.

"Wow," Deanna said. She had moved in beside me while I had been speaking with Miss Curvy. "Where do you suppose they build them like that?"

"I don't know, but I'm thinking of moving there."

Deanna shoved me in protest. She succeeded in forcing me to shift my weight from one foot to the other.

Without her stripper shoes, Deanna didn't quite come up to my shoulder. The shoes made the difference between Oh-my-God statuesque, and Oh-my-God cute.

When Arianna disappeared into the crowd, Deanna handed me her work bag and said; "Come on, walk me to my car."

Four o'clock in the morning, and it was still a good ninety degrees out: Summertime in Vegas. It wasn't just the temperature that had me sweating.

Deanna had put her hair up in a clip and was wearing a light summer dress, a pair of wedge sandals, and a thin gold chain around her neck. That was it. I had hugged her good night enough times to know she never wore underwear leaving work. I supposed if I had been wearing a sequined g-string all night, I would appreciate the breathing room also.

I scanned the parking lot as she led the way to her car. Deanna never used valet at work, even after the incident. She said it was because one day she was going to kidnap me and take me away from all this. I think it was because she was too smart to let Tim, the valet, touch her car.

Deanna drove a next model year silver Lexus. I was driving a timeless 1980 Dodge pickup. A matter of taste, I suppose.

She chirped her car open, and I dropped the work bag full of costumes, hair drier, makeup, and other mysterious tools of her trade in the trunk, and pressed it closed.

She was waiting for me by her open driver's door. She stood on her toes and hugged me good night and tucked something into the front pocket of my slacks. It would be a generous denomination. It always was, and it was never necessary. Anyone would have paid for the privilege of a few minutes in her presence. I was no exception. She kissed my cheek and looked into my eyes. Then she got in behind the wheel and drove away.

"God damn," I said to no one at all.


"What the hell is wrong with that guy?"

"I'd of got a blowjob, not some lame ass peck on the cheek."

"No doubt. The guy's got to be a fag."

"Check out the video."

"Play it back."

"Let me rewind it."

"Look at that, look at that... I don't think she's wearing any underwear."

"Oh, shit. back it up. freeze that. Oh shit."

"Now, that's what I'm talking about."

"Print me up a copy of that. God damn."

"I thought you didn't like being out here in the

van."

"Shut up and play that back again."


I circled back around to the front of the club, took one quick look at the parking lot, and checked my watch; 4:14, and about 41...42 seconds. I had forty five minutes and eighteen seconds to go before I was off. I would have to deal with it.

"Tim, Tim, what are these cabs doing parked across the driveway?"

Tim answered the way he always did. He shrugged. He went back to talking through the car window to the two entertainers who had just gotten off work.

"Tim," I shouted, "tell them about your cock later. Get these god damn cabs out of the driveway, now."

Tim nodded at the girls he was talking to, as if I had just confirmed the rumor about the size of his penis, he had no doubt been relating when I interrupted him. Everyone had heard the rumor of Tim's nine inch dick. It was hard not to have heard. It was practically the second thing out of Tim's mouth after you first met him; "Hi, I'm Tim...."

It didn't surprise me that Tim was generously endowed. It surprised me that he could find that monster with both hands and a map: The kid was dumb as a rock.

Tim began shouting at cabdrivers to move their cabs. Cookie was in a shouting match all his own.

"Look you fat fucker, I counted three guys out of your cab. Three," he held up three, insulin bloated fingers, "count them, three."

"Kiss my ass, you steroid freak," the cabdriver

countered. "I can count, all the way to five. You should learn." He spoke intelligible English. He was Caucasian: Rare.

"Norm, I'm gonna kill...," Cookie began.

I snatched the seventy-five dollars from Cookie's hand and shoved it into the hand of the cabdriver. I took the cabdriver by the shoulders, turned him around and began walking him toward the cab line. "Have a great night, sir," I said.

The cabdriver resisted. He leaned back against my pressure. He was probably close to three hundred pounds, but it was a soft three hundred pounds, all doughnuts and 7-11 sandwiches. I kept the pressure on and kept him walking. Probably the most strenuous exercise he ever got was getting his bulk in and out of his cab.

"Don't touch me," the cabdriver protested. "You can't touch me."

"Can't or shouldn't, sir?" I asked. We kept moving.

"You can't touch me. Get your hands off me. That's assault."

"Actually, I am touching you, so, obviously, I can. And it's battery. Touching is battery."

When the cabdriver realized I wasn't going to take my hands off his back, and he wasn't going to be able to stop our progress any way short of falling to the ground, he began walking on his own. I let him waddle away from me.

"I'll sue the shit out of you."

"Of course you will sir. Have a great day," I said. I checked my watch again. 4:19, and twelve seconds. Just Forty minutes and forty eight seconds....

I slipped inside the club and squatted down against the wall to stretch my knees and back. I was getting a little old be be arguing with degenerate cabdrivers and explaining to fifty-year-old men that topless women in a topless bar, were working, not socializing, and they needed to be paid for their work. I was far to young to be feeling this old.

Most of the time, I could have done my job with a prerecorded message, or a set of flash cards: "Sir, how many dances did you get?" "Sir, you owe the girl $20.00 for each dance." Sir, I'm sure she really does like you, but you still need to pay her." Sir, pay the girl, or I will beat you to a bloody pulp." "Thank you, sir."

I had seen a girl do it once, come in to work with a set of cards with her questions and responses. It was classic. She made a bundle that night. "Hi, my name is Brooke, what's yours?" "Wow, that's the most interesting thing I've ever heard." "Would you like a dance?" "No, I would not like to go (home, hotel, out, dinner, coffee...) with you." "No, not even for (fill in the blank) dollars." "Thank you. Have a great night." "Norm, throw this guy out."

Sometimes Rick would introduce me to an irate customer as the Head Doorman, whatever that meant. Whenever he did that, I knew he didn't want to be bothered with the customer complaint. He would introduce me, then walk away, leaving me to my own devices. It generally meant the customer would be leaving.

The title of Head Doorman didn't come with any extra pay or perks, but I didn't mind too much. It would do until the head of security position came available, again. I liked having the opportunity to run security my way. At least I knew it was getting done right. The pain of it was, it left very little time to make any real money. Robert hustled tables all night, at 20 dollars and up per seat. Big John had a lock on working the VIP room, where the real money was. The other guys scavenged money where they could; strong-arming, extorting, finders fees from girls for high-rolling customers.... I made most my money collecting delinquent lap dance debts, and being a shoulder to cry on: It was a living.

I pushed myself back to my feet without audibly screaming in pain, and saw Robert point at me from across the room. He was talking to a little red-faced customer. Robert grinned and I thought I read his lips saying something like; "head doorman." I checked my watch.

"I just got ripped off," the red faced customer said when he was within ten feet of me. I nodded my head and looked around for Kevin. On second thought, the customer was still conscious, and didn't appear to be bleeding, so he probably wasn't talking about Kevin.

"How did you get ripped off, sir?" I asked.

"I'm out $250 dollars," he stammered.

"I didn't ask how much, sir. I asked, how."

"What do you mean?"

"I mean, were you sitting there, minding your own business, and a girl started doing dances for you, then asked you to pay her?" There was no recognition from Red Face, so I guessed again. "Did the waitress ring up a bunch of drinks on your credit card that you never ordered?" Nothing. "Did someone knock you down and steal your wallet..." I wasn't having much luck. I kept trying. "Did you pay for a bottle of Crystal and it tasted like Moet? Did a bouncer not get you a place to sit after he took your money to get you one...?" If he was going to make me guess I could be at this all morning, I thought. I kept going down the list. "Was your credit card over charged? Did the ATM only give you back fifty dollars and a receipt that said you got three hundred? Did a girl tell you she would meet you somewhere if you gave her half up front...?" His face lit up. Aah, standard scam number 41B: The old bait the moron with something illegal, then blow him off.

"A girl told you she would meet you at your hotel room after work, if you paid her 250 dollars up front, and the rest when she got there, and now you can't find her anywhere, right?" I confirmed.

The customer's face got a deeper shade of red, and his eyes darted down and to the left several times. I was sure it hadn't sounded nearly so transparent, or stupid in his own mind. I saved him the trouble of trying to think up a lie.

"Sir, soliciting prostitution is illegal in Las Vegas. Now, you can call a cop and try and explain it to him, or you write it off as a 250 dollar lesson." I knew what his answer would be even before he fully digested what I was telling him. I left him standing there, and went searching for Lori.

"She already checked out and went home," Savvy answered my query. "Did you need to talk to her?"

"Yea, remind me tomorrow to talk to her about something."

"Bait and switch?" Savvy asked.

I nodded.

JB was in the corner of the dressing room testing

the pliability of a pair of swollen new breast implants on an entertainer with a bad case of acne. The skin over the implants was so tight, it shined. It looked painful to me, having that much foreign material stuffed under you skin. They looked uncomfortable from the other side too; looked like you could chip a tooth on one. None of that seemed to bother JB, or the entertainer. JB rubbed, and massaged for all he was worth. He looked like a kid deciding between two footballs; which he liked better.

I checked my watch and exited the dressing room: Eleven minutes, nine seconds. I had to get to the office and start on the night's incident reports.

The "pay me now, I'll meet you later" scam had Lori written all over it. I would forget about it by tomorrow. I knew Savvy would remind me.

Savvy was the weekend House Mom. She had been an entertainer, about two hundred pounds ago. She handled everything in the dressing room that needed handling; makeup, costumes, squabbles, gripes, complaints...from falling-down-drunk twenty year old girls, to forgotten combinations on lockers. She was sweet, and rotund, and calm, and nothing ever seemed to get by her. She was everything you needed to handle a dressing room full of high-strung topless entertainers. Lord knows I couldn't have done it.

I waved to Big John on my way past the VIP room. I noticed his pockets were bulging.

I saw Kevin and Robert on each arm of a semi-conscious drunk customer, dragging him toward the side exit.

I peeked out the front doors of the club and saw a traffic jam of taxicabs, and heard Cookie arguing with a cabdriver about the amount of the bribe.

I ducked into the office.

The morning crew was in the office prepping for their shift. I picked an empty spot on the edge of a small desk and started in on the incident reports; four beatings (customer disputes), two over-doses (one customer, and one entertainer). Two taxicab fender benders in the parking lot...everything else could be effectively covered up without a report, I thought.

By the time I had finished the reports, the office was nearly as crowded and noisy as the club had been. JB bragged about his sexual exploits from the night. Big John laughed about how much money he had made. Kevin laughed about the customers he had beaten up. Bartenders, bar-backs and cocktail waitresses complained about cheap customers. Robert sat, smiling, and took it all in.

I looked over the reports. I would have to sit down and write the Great American Novel, one day. I was getting some great practice.


I woke the same way I always do, with the nightmare of a phone ringing, and a sleep-deprivation hangover. This time the hangover was worse, and the phone suddenly stopped ringing.

I heard Susan's muted voice from downstairs, then her bare feet coming up the stairs.

I waited. My temples throbbed, and there was a crushing weight pressing outward from behind my eyes. I used the palms of my hands to press them back inward. I smelled something terrible. It was me.

Susan gently poked her head into the room. "It's Rick."

This was it. Exactly how the nightmare always went.

Susan handed me the phone and I cleared my throat. Something thick and viscous was coating the entire inside of my mouth. I forced out a "what?" I sounded like hell.

"What happened last night?" Rick asked. He didn't sound so good himself.

"It's too early for guessing games, boss. What do you want."

"Well, I'm down here with detective Pike, from Metro. There was an incident with a cabdriver?"

"That narrows it down."

"What?"

"Nothing," I grumbled. I knew which one he meant. "No one got hurt."

"Why don't you come down her and explain that to the detective?"

"Because it's like..." I checked the digital alarm clock beside my bed. "eight thirty in the morning," I said.

"I got the call at seven thirty," Rick said. His voice was becoming testy. I couldn't blame him. If I got testy, this would be doing it for me.

"I'll be down in about an hour," I said and hung up.

"Are you fired?" Susan asked.

"I don't know yet." I sat up over the edge of the bed and steadied myself against the spinning of the room.

Susan stood between my legs and massaged my shoulders and neck. I let my head hang loose as she manipulated the muscles that popped like bowstrings under her fingers. She had strong hands. I started to fade out. I shook myself awake and gently pushed Susan away. I didn't want to feel any better than I did. I wanted to be in pain this morning. The pain reminded me why I needed to get out of this business.

Susan kissed the top of my head. "There's coffee ready when you get downstairs," she said as she pulled open the heavy drapes that effectively blacked out the bedroom's window. Bright morning light stabbed at my eyes through my clenched lids. Vegas morning light. It was brighter than normal light. More intense: Meaner.

"I'll get you an ice bag," Susan sighed, noting my freshly dotted eye.

"And some aspirin," I shouted after her.

I might have fallen asleep under the shower. I dressed in a pair of faded, once black jeans, boots and a light t-shirt with no logo, and stood in the kitchen drinking black coffee. I didn't want to sit down. If I sat down, I wouldn't get back up.

It occurred to me that it was Sunday. Left to my own devices, I would have slept until about ten thirty, showered and laid on the couch and watched pre-season football for most of the day. Susan would have rubbed my feet, and I would have faded in and out of consciousness until the afternoon games started rotating in all their third string players. I would have gotten in a couple hours worth of workout, got some dinner, and then crawled back in bed and let Susan rub my feet until I fell asleep. My alarm would have gone off at seven fifty-one P.M., and I would have been to work by nine. Not a perfect day, but pretty much as good as it got.

Now, I would talk to a cop, be talked to by Rick, and if I still had a job afterward, my day would be shot. I would be too tired to train, too tired to watch football, too tired to eat. I would get home, crawl back into bed, pissed off at the world, and pass out. I would wake up to the nightmare of a phone ringing, with no idea where I was or what time it was. Despite Susan's best efforts, I would go to work with a shit attitude, and chances were, someone would get hurt.

I finished my coffee, and headed down to Brass Poles.


Detective Pike was a cop; he dressed like a cop, he sat like a cop, he spoke like a cop: condescending, superior, disinterested. There were two other detectives with him, one of them presumably a woman. They weren't introduced. I didn't care.

"A Martin Issacs filed a battery complaint against the club last night. He claims you shoved him in the back and he twisted his knee," Detective Pike said.

I looked at Pike. He was a a fairly big man, bigger than me. He had clean features, well groomed. The blazer he wore was cheap. His nose was straight and his ears weren't cauliflowered. He probably wouldn't last six seconds with me on the ground, I thought.

Everyone in the room—the three cops and Rick—were staring at me. I stared back.

"Well?" Detective Pike said.

"That's the first question you've asked," I said.

The other detective's jaw dropped open a little. The

female detective grinned. Pike cocked his head, like he hadn't quite heard me right.

"Norm," Rick warned. "Did you put it in last night's reports?"

My head hurt. I looked at detective Pike. He was standing over me in the standard cop take-a-superior-position technique. I was seated in one of the leather rockers. From right there, I could probably do a single leg takedown on him. Pop his knee—hurt him permanent—before the other cops could pull me off.

"You know, we have other witnesses," Pike said.

"Well, that's lucky, because I don't recall anything about it," I said.

Pike looked at Rick. Rick shrugged.

"Cookie should be in in about a half an hour," Rick said.

I smiled. I knew what that meant. Cookie would have already told Rick about the incident over the phone. He would come in here and spill his guts to the cops, telling them anything and everything they wanted to hear, or could direct him to say. Cookie was a spineless little bitch, I thought. That's why I kept him at the front door with the cabdrivers and Tim the valet. I didn't want him knowing what went on inside the club. I would have fired him if I had the authority, but apparently that was out of the "Head Doorman's" realm. Rick had mentioned it to give me the opportunity to tell my side first. I didn't have a side to tell.

"I'm sure Cookie will be able to help you guys," I said to the cops in general. "Rick, I've only had about two and a half hours sleep."

Rick took it from there. "Look guys, he had to work last night. You know, I'm surprised he can remember his own name right now, you know?" Pike never took his eyes off me. Rick was in full politician mode. "Why don't you let him go home, get some sleep, and when he comes in tonight, we'll go over the reports again, he'll probably remember something, okay?"

Pike just stared at me some more. The two other detectives stood from their perches on the desks, like they were ready to wrap it up.

"Slow week, huh?" I asked detective Pike.

"Okay, okay..." Rick said and took me by the arm, encouraging me to stand up. "Go home, get some sleep. See if you can remember anything about a cabdriver. We'll see you at nine, right?"

I smiled at Pike and left the office.

Rick poked his head out after me. "By the way, what happened to our eye?"

"Nothin'," I said, "They've always been blue." I went home.

"Do you have to go in tonight?" Susan asked.

"Yep," I said.

"I'm sorry," she said.

It was her way of letting me know she would be okay with my getting fired. She would be okay with my just not going in to work one night. I appreciated it.

I always imagined that's how my job with Brass Poles would end. One night, I would be sitting on the couch, watching TV, one eye on the clock, waiting for eight-thirty: time to leave for work. One day, I would just continue to sit there.

I had worked eight different strip clubs over the past eighteen years, and I had never quit a single one. I had been fired from every club I had worked in my life, since I got out of the army at 21. Every night I thought about that as I watched the clock creep toward eight thirty. Every night I got up and went to work.

I fell asleep on the couch, with Susan rubbing my feet, listening to a 6 to 3 Chargers, Niners pre-season third quarter score.


"Just give me the Readers Digest version, please. I'll read the full report later."

"Yes, sir. Agent Marquez successfully installed two listening devices in the target's office at 1221 Remar Way..."

"Tell me she didn't B&E it."

No, sir. We enlisted the assistance of the locals, a Metro detective Pike, to gain legal and warranted access."

"You brought local law in without my authorization?"

"Sir, local law remains unaware of our purpose for the request. There was an opportunity, a police report filed that morning. The detective was going in to do interviews anyway. We just piggybacked."

"I guess that's all right. Where else are we listening?"

"We've got their cell phones, or course. We've got the OnStar systems."

"All of them?"

"Every one."

"Good work."

"We are maintaining the on-site listening post also."

"Do we need it? It's a little redundant, don't you think?"

"There's a lot of talk in the parking lots."

"Yea, but how much of it relevant? I mean, we've got the phones, cars, office now. It's expensive to maintain the on-site."

"Didn't we get the funding?"

"We got it. That's a good point. We might as well use it. Keep the on-site post."

"Yes sir."

"I wish you had used the local law we had already recruited instead of that other detective, though."

"Pike?"

"Yea. Our guy's vice. I think we could have found a reason to get Marquez in the office with him."

"Yes sir, but detective Pike was going in anyway on a battery complaint. It was a 7 a.m. opportunity. I just thought...."

"No, you did fine. It will be fine. We just don't want to bring their metro unit into the loop if we don't absolutely have to. I mean, I'm guessing there's a lot of potential for contamination of the locals in something like this."

"Yes sir. We're seeing evidence of that. Mostly off-duty stuff, but we're hearing some of the vice officers may be on the take also."

"That's what I'm hearing from our source too."

"Would you like to start a file?"

"Oh, lord no. The last thing we need to do is muddy this whole thing with an investigation of their police department. Indicting a strip club owner and the city council, is one thing. Bringing indictments against a dozen local law enforcement is something else completely."

"A couple hundred..."

"That bad? In any case. We need to stay focused."

"I agree sir."

"Good. Keep your people together. Keep them sharp. I may have a gift for us in a couple of weeks that will bust this whole thing wide open for us."

"Did we get access to The Act?"

"Just...keep your people sharp, and keep that rumor under control, for now. I don't want anyone getting complacent. Tell your people, good work. It's coming together."

"Yes sir. Thank you sir."


"How much does the scumbag want?"

"Ten grand ought to do it," Terry said.

"Cock suckers," Joey growled. He went into the open safe, and pulled out one banded stack of hundred dollar bills. He tossed it to Terry.

Terry bobbled the cash before getting a handle on it. He shoved it into the inner pocket of his sport coat.

Lisa Marie, who had been engrossed in a men's magazine across the office, stared in incredulous, gaped-mouthed horror.

Joey saw the look and returned her stare with a angry look of his own.

She slapped the magazine shut and hurled it like a limp frisbee across the room at Joey.

Terry looked over his shoulder to where the magazine had come from, then to where it had gone. He looked confused. The exchange, if not the magazine, had gone over his head. "Okay, well, I'll get this out to Kerry," Terry babbled. Joey ignored him.

Terry left the office. Lisa Marie exploded in a torrent of profanity. "What the fuck, Joey. You give that fucking guy ten fucking grand and I can't even get a new fucking car!"

"Shut the fuck up," Joey said. "You're driving a fucking Bentley. What the fuck are you complaining about?"

"You gonna give it to me?"

"Shit," Joey scoffed.

Why the fuck you got to give him ten fucking grand for?" Lisa Marie pouted.

"So I can keep the city council off my fucking back. What the fuck do you think?"

She clicked her tongue and huffed and snatched another magazine off the desk and tossed it in a random direction.

"Quit being such a cunt," Joey said. "You think I like paying those assholes?" He put some papers through his shredder. "Every month there's something."

"Can't you just...I don't know...do something?"

"I am doing something. I'm paying them to quit fucking with me. Don't I pay you for the same thing?"

"Fuck you Joey," Lisa Marie spat. "Why don't you get a lawyer, or something?"

"I've got a fucking lawyer. Last time I let him handle it, we lost all our girls under 21. Remember? That's why you can't work."

"Fuck you. I work."

"What the fuck do you do?"

"You try sucking your dick."

"Good point," Joey grinned. He mumbled under his breath. "Like that's worth ten grand."

"What?" Lisa Marie asked.

"Nothing," Joey said.


"Kim,"

"Terry,"

"I got something for you."

Councilperson Kerry licked her lips and watched Terry's hand go into his coat. She watched him pull out a thick stack of hundred dollar bills bound with a rubber band.

Terry handed the money over. "Here you go, five grand. I told you I'd come through."

"Thank you, thank you, thank you." Councilperson Kerry simpered. "Thank you Jesus."

"You can just call me Terry," Terry said. "Don't thank me, thank Joey with your vote."

The councilperson shot him a sideways look. It was hard to take her eyes off the cash. "Don't I always do the right thing?" the councilperson said. "I do want to thank Joey though."

"Go ahead," Terry said.

I'm not calling him from my phone. They check

records."

"Use my cell," Terry said and handed Kerry his phone. "just don't mention any numbers, okay."

"I'm not stupid, Terry."


"A big screen?" I asked. I wondered if I had heard her right.

"Yea. 47 inch Sony plasma," Deanna confirmed. "He thought we were going there for a new swim suit."

"Where do you shop where you can get a swim suit and a plasma TV? Joe's bikini's and TV's?" I wondered aloud.

"Forum Shops, silly," Deanna said. She was straightening my collar, brushing lint off my shirt, letting her hands drift wherever they wanted. Pretty much where I wanted too. "He was late and I saw him coming in, looking around for me at Spago's. So I pretended like I was mad. Like I was leaving."

"How late was he?" I asked to prolong the conversation, and Deanna's fidgeting with my clothes. She was just beginning to get to the interesting parts.

"About five minutes," Deanna said.

I choked. "I'll bet that cost him." I tried not to sound too sarcastic. It wasn't easy.

Deanna smiled at my reaction. "About six," she said.

"Six...thousand," I asked. Deanna was nodding her acknowledgement. "dollars?"

She nodded some more. "You want it?" She was gently scratching my nipples with her fingernails now. My comprehension level was dropping exponentially.

"Want what?"

"The TV."

"Do I want your new Sony 46 inch plasma TV?"

"47 inch," she corrected. "It's really nice."

I laughed. "I'm sure it is," I said. "I can just see me trying to explain that one to Susan. 'Hi honey, This beautiful twenty two year old stripper had this extra TV. She thought we might want it.'"

Deanna was tucking my shirt into my pants now. There was less room down there than there had been a minute before. "Well," she said, "you could always come over to my place to watch it."

"Just plop down in your living room and watch the game," I said.

"Actually, this one goes in the bedroom. I have a really nice one in the living room."

I sighed heavily and pulled her hands out of my pants. "Jesus Christ, Deanna. You're killing me." I held her hands and kissed one of them.

She smiled. "Why do you have to be in love?"

"Just my bad luck, I guess," I said.

She bit one of my knuckles, like a playful kitten, and walked away into the human morass of the club.

"I think she likes you," Robert said from behind me. He was forever sneaking up on me like that.

"What's not to like?" I sighed.

"Oops, got to go," Robert said.

I looked and saw Rick coming toward me. He was being followed by what looked like a shaved Silverback gorilla wearing a Golds Gym tee-shirt, and a baggy pair of

Golds Gym sweat pants that might have doubled as an extermination tent.

"Hey, boss, I don't remember anything more about that cabdriver incident." I said.

"Don't worry about that. I got that covered," Rick said. He looked at me closely. It made me nervous. "This is Tony."

I shook hands with the Golds Gym billboard.

"He's Mike's new head of security."

My hand involuntarily clenched tighter on Tony's. I looked at Rick.

Rick's look told me it was not his idea. Apologetic. It didn't make me any happier. I let go of Tony's hand.

"I need you to show him around. Let him know what's what, you know," Rick said.

"I think I got it," Tony said.

His accent was heavy East coast. New York, I thought, but then, what did I know. I was just a fucking bouncer.

"He's got it Rick," I said.

"Do me a favor, okay?"

I nodded. It's not like I hadn't done it before—trained a new head of security—five times.

Rick left us.

I swallowed my pride like a hot chunk of greasy asphalt. "So, where are you from?" I asked.

"New York," Tony said. He was looking off toward the stage.

The girl on stage was lazing her way around the pole. Not much to look at. Tony seemed entranced.

"Where'd you work? Scores, Rick's, Flash

Dancers..."

Tony didn't answer. He kept looking at the girl on stage. I started looking too. Maybe I was missing something.

The song stopped. The girl on stage began putting her clothes back on, and Tony finally remembered I was standing beside him. "How much you make off these whores a night," he asked.

I looked at his chin, the well trimmed beard, and thought how good my fist would feel against it. "Excuse me?" I said.

Tony shrugged. He had either lost interest, or had forgotten his question. He was watching the next girl take the stage and shuck her top. "Whadda ya weigh?" he asked me. "About 210?" He hadn't taken his eyes off the girl on stage. I hadn't taken my eyes off his chin. "You ever think about gettin' a little bigger, I could hook you up."

"Excuse me for a minute," I said. I made a b-line to the office.

I rapped my knuckles on the door probably harder than I should have. Rick opened the door. I pushed past him into the office. Joey was sitting behind his desk, shredding papers.

"What the fuck, Joey?" I said.

"What's your problem." Joey never looked up. I was pretty sure he already knew what my problem was.

"Why am I training a new head of security?"

"You want me to have Robert do it?"

"Norm," Rick said from behind me.

"This guy's never worked in a strip club before, has he?"

"Norm," Rick tried again.

"So?" Joey said.

So. I had never thought of it like that. How was I supposed to respond to, so?

Rick put his hand on my shoulder. "Norm. Just relax. You're next in line."

"How long have I worked for you?" I asked Joey.

"A little too long, maybe," Joey said.

"Come on Joey," Rick said, "Norm's a good guy."

"Maybe you're right," I said to Joey. "Maybe ten years is too long. And how many days have I missed in those ten years?"

"You missed those three days over Super Bowl weekend," Joey reminded me.

"I was in jail, Joey, remember? That cabbie and his buddies tried to take Cookie's head off with a shovel."

Joey grinned in memory. He never stopped his shredding. "And you did me a favor by stopping them?"

Rick moved between me and Joey to keep me from crawling over the desk. "Norm, come on out here and talk to me." He had both hands on both of my shoulders.

"What do I got to do?" I asked Joey.

Joey finally stopped shredding and looked up. "Can you get me a vice cop to tell me when all the raids are going to be?"

I didn't answer.

"Can you?" Joey asked again. His voice was rising in timber and volume with each word. "I didn't think so. Until you can do that, I'll hire any cocksucker I want for head of security. Got that?"

Rick kept his hands on my shoulders. He was a big

man, but if I wanted over that desk, I was getting over it. "Come on," Rick said. He guided me to the back door of the office. I walked out in front of him.

It was hot out. It didn't help my mood. "What the fuck?" It was about as articulate as I was capable of at that moment.

"Look, Norm. You're going to be head of security. You're next in line. I swear. Joey knows you run security. He knows. This is just a special situation."

"No shit," I said. "It's always a special situation."

"Just hang lose," Rick said. "Joey'll get tired of this guy in a couple months. You know how he is."

"Yea, I know how he is."

Rick thumped me hard on the back. "Come on, lets go back inside."

"I'm going to hang out here for a few minutes," I said.

Rick left me alone in the parking lot.


The office buzz that night was all about Tony, or Big Tony, as he had introduced himself to everyone in the club. No one had given him a tour of the club. It was a joke anyway. We would never see the guy. He would poke his head in the club every once in a while. Maybe fire someone at the security meetings. He would hire his own flake steroid-stallion friends, and generally be no more annoying than a nasty case of hemorids. Just like every other head of security for the past few years.

JB said he was a cop, undercover.

Big John said he didn't think so. He had bought

some great Chinese growth hormone, and some testosterone from him already.

Cookie and Kevin said the guy was cool. He was going to get them free Golds memberships.

Robert said the guy was an idiot.

I didn't have anything to say at all. I sat in the office and wrote my own incident reports and let everyone else write their own. It was childish, I know, I was pouting. Neener, neener, neener on them.

"Settle down people. I have a special announcement. Settle down. We got approval. We are employing section 314 of the Patriot Act."

"We got the Act?"

"Settle down. Settle down, people. We got the Act. That means we've got everything we want on this guy. Bank accounts, wire transfers, phones, mail...everything, so start digging."

"We've got his phones already."

"I want everything. I want to know what he sings in the shower. I want to know how many sheets of toilet paper he uses."

"Credit card records?"

"Everything."

"On everybody?"

"Everything on everybody."

"Well, what can't we go after?"

"Now I know we haven't had an opportunity to look over the Act, or its provisions, but so far, what I've heard, nothing is off limits. Now, that being said, the FBI has ever used the Act in this sort of investigation before. This is a first. So follow established procedure the best you can.

"I've been over the Act a little. It's pretty open. Not much we can't do."

"Reasonable suspicion?"

"Not necessary. We don't even need warrants."

"No warrants?"

"Not as far as I know."

"All right. I want everybody to take a copy of section 314 home with them before they leave today. Look it over. See what you can find. This is a precedent setter. Make us look good."


Two months, Rick had guessed Tony would last. Then I was next in line for the head of security position. Rick had made that prediction just over two years ago. I was still waiting.

Joey Rizoli was getting ready to open a new club—the biggest, most expensive strip club ever built—and everyone wanted a piece. Brass Poles had degenerated into a pathetic dance of pandering to every local politician, developer and city official in Vegas.

A councilperson, or one of their cronies would come in nearly every night, acting the fool, demanding special privileges, breaking every law on the books, and there was nothing we could do about it.

The office change safe, with it's bundles of cash wrapped in the names of the city council members, left little room for the register banks. Police officers, fire marshal, health inspectors, building inspectors, licensing agents, judges, lawyers, and it seemed, everyone else who owned a suit and tie in the city, were in and out of the office at all hours, day and night. Not one of them we could touch. They could get naked and stand on a table and crow like a rooster, and all I could do was move to the other side of the room and curse the lack of fortitude that kept me coming to work.

The club had become the wild west. It was every man for himself: Beat what you could out of the customers. Coerce what you could out of the entertainers. Steal what you could from the cabbies.

The high-rollers had abandoned the club. The watered-down drinks, violence, and overly-aggressive prostitutes drove them away. The top-end entertainers had followed the highrollers to greener pastures. We were left with the degenerates and losers and dealers and pimps and politicians.

Prostitutes, once shunned by the club, lounged on the couches by the front door, annoying the legitimate entertainers and waiting for their opportunity to perform an "office party" for the constant flow of city officials who paid Joey Rizoli visits, nightly.

Rick had become the Brass Poles pimp. He glad-handed politicians and rounded up prostitutes and cleaned up the office after. He didn't look any more thrilled about working at the club than I did. He stopped promising me the head of security position. We both knew it would never happen. He barely spoke with me, or anyone else at all. He stood in the DJ booth with his jaw clenched, and looked over what had become of his life.

Joey Rizoli himself had become one miserable son-of-a-bitch. He smiled in the faces of the lawmakers, and cursed them to hell, behind their backs. He resented the fact that his club had been transformed into a city-employee brothel. If Rick had become the club's pimp, Joey had become it's madam.

It was too late to turn back. He was two years and thirteen million dollars into construction on the new club, and it was only half built. It seemed there was no end to the inspections. No end to the licensing hearings. No end to the out-held hands. A five thousand dollar bribe here, ten thousand there, free comps to anyone with a badge...it was nothing. It had become part of doing business.

Joey Rizoli had sold his soul for the new club, and there was no getting it back.

"I don't believe this. Nothing. This is what we've got? Nothing?"

"Extortion, wire fraud, conspiracy to commit..."

"Nothing. That's what it all adds up to. Do you have any idea what this operation cost? Two and a half years, twenty three agents, full surveillance.... What did we spend on that Cambina idiot, alone? $100,000 a year, for two and a half years?"

"Twenty seven months sir."

"Twenty seven months. Ten thousand hours of audio tapes that I had to listen to...mother F-er this and mother F-er that. A thousand hours of video tapes of cars pulling in and out of the parking lot. Some slobs getting the hell kicked out of them...low grade porn...I don't believe this."

"Sir, I talked to the prosecutor. We can get indictments all the way around. Rizoli, five council members in both cities..."

"On what?"

"Bribery, wire fraud..."

"Don't...just don't.... You know what Manowski is working on right now? They're onto a potential al Qaeda sleeper cell. Yea, that's right. That's what they're working on. What do I have? I have bribery of a city official."

"Sir, we can stay on it."

"Why? We can't even employ the RICO act on most of this stuff. This is useless. I want it taken down now."

"Sir?"

"Break it down. Break the whole thing down, now. Reassign your people. Put that Cambina idiot somewhere where you can keep an eye on him, and get me the heck out of this godforsaken city."

"Abandon the investigation, sir?"

"Lord Jesus, Mary and Joseph, no. I didn't say abandon the investigation. Cut our losses. Take what we've got and run with it. Hand it over to the prosecutors, whatever we've got."

"I'm sorry sir."

"It's not your fault. Hey, we got article 314 employed for the first time. We set a precedent. It will come in handy in the future. Even it it was for an extortion and bribery case. Nothing huh? No drugs, money laundering...nothing?"

"Sorry sir."

"Forget it. When can your people be ready to go?"

"The raid? They've been ready."

"Great. Tomorrow morning, then. I can't wait to get back home."

I sat on the couch and watched the second hand sweep and the minute hand click its way toward 8:30.

"I can't do this anymore."

I didn't get an answer. Susan had been in San Diego taking care of her mother for months. Kiko had nothing to say about my comment. I got up and headed to work.

I hadn't had anyone pull a gun on me in over a year. This kid didn't really want to kill me. He just wanted to scare me, I thought. But I wished he wasn't pointing the damn thing at me either way.

I stood there looking down the business end of the shotgun the kid had pulled from the trunk of his car. It looked like you could park a limo in there. A big one. One of those stretch jobs. That's what I got for being a nice guy.

I had tossed the kid for bringing in his own bottle of booze. Not really a big deal. The floor was littered with them at the end of the night. Just don't get caught, was all I asked. This kid got caught, he and his buddy. I had just walked them out. I hadn't spanked them or anything. I guess I did laugh a little when he told me he was going to come back and kill me. I guess he didn't like being laughed at. Now he was pointing that goddamn Mossberg at me, and his buddy was egging him on.

"Shoot the mutherfucker."

"I'm gonna shoot you mutherfucker."

"Shoot 'em. Shoot the muther fucker."

"Mutherfucker, I'm gonna shoot you."

I figured they would get around to it pretty soon. Work themselves into it. I was damned if they were going to shoot me in the back though. There was no way I could get close enough to this kid to take it away from him. That had been my second mistake. Once I got them out to the parking lot, I had let them walk the rest of the way to their car all by themselves. I should have walked with them. He would have never got into the trunk if I had. I was getting old, I thought. The thought made me smile. Ironic: It was looking like I wouldn't have to worry about that much longer.

Someone had gone inside and told about me and the kid with the shotgun, because we were starting to draw a crowd. Rubberneckers were piling out of the bar to watch me die. I couldn't say I blamed them. I had been a royal prick lately.

Robert came outside. He moved like he always did; like he knew exactly where he was headed, but he was in no special rush to get there. He walked, that easy way, right between me and the kid with the gun.

"Hey, Norm."

"Robert," I said, "you might want to move a little to the left." It was a good line to go out on, but I didn't sound near as much like Clint Eastwood as I had hoped. My sneer was no where near as cool either, I knew.

The kid was still pointing the gun at me, but now anything that came out of it would have to go through Robert first.

Robert turned and smiled at the kids. "Norm, are you bothering these gentlemen?"

The kids looked confused. They stopped shouting "kill the mutherfucker," for a second. But just for a second.

"I'm gonna kill that mutherfucker. Get out of the way, mutherfucker."

"You mean me or him?" Robert asked.

"Robert, get out of the way," I said.

The kids looked even more confused.

Robert didn't look like someone you wanted to shoot. He was handsome and smiling and friendly. He looked like a guy you would trust dating your sister, not someone you wanted to kill out in a parking lot of a Vegas titty bar at four in the morning. It must have registered with the kids, because they didn't seem as intent on killing anybody anymore.

We were sort of stuck. I wasn't about to turn and walk away. Robert wasn't about to get out of the way. The kids were not about to put the gun down and drive away either. Niles solved the problem for us.

Niles was a customer, of sorts. Actually, he just came down to hang out with Big John some nights. He didn't buy anything. He didn't drink anything. He didn't say much of anything. He mostly leaned on a wall of the VIP room and talked to Big John. I wouldn't go as far as to say Niles was a shady individual, but unlike Robert, he wasn't someone you wanted dating your sister, either.

Niles had casually walked around behind the two kids, and had casually stuck the barrel of a small pistol in the ear of the kid with the shotgun. "Y'all fucking suck at this," Niles said. I couldn't tell if he was talking to the kids, or to me. I didn't much care. The kid lowered the shotgun.

Robert took the shotgun away from the kid. Niles kept his gun in the kid's ear. I took a full breath.

I was getting old. The first time a kid had pointed a gun at me in the parking lot of a titty bar, twenty years ago. I had laughed at him. I had called him names and had belittled him for all I was worth, trying to get him to pull the trigger. He hadn't pulled the trigger. He had started crying and had gotten in his car and drove away. I had seen him a couple years later down at the beach, and he had apologized to me. I wouldn't have recognized him if he hadn't said something about it. He said he had been in a twelve step program and this was one of the steps. I accept his apology and told him it was all right, and he had cried again.

I didn't think I would be shaking hands with this kid in the future. I think if I had said word one to him, he would have shot me, and I would have died in that parking lot, and given Susan one more thing to grieve. I was glad he didn't shoot me. I was getting old.

We told the kids to take off and we gave Niles the shotgun. We figured he had earned it. Robert and I went back inside and went back to work.

Half the club hadn't heard about the incident, and couldn't have cared less, if they had. Beautiful near-naked twenty-year-olds could do that for you.

I spent my last hour depressed. I wasn't afraid to die, I knew, but I hadn't chased it either. Twenty years ago, I had nothing to live for. Now it was different. My time was done. The job had passed me by. Somewhere along the line I had earned something to live for.

Now the clubs wanted good-looking college kids

who wouldn't provoke someone into pulling a gun on them, and certainly wouldn't think of standing there to get shot if someone did. I was a liability. I was a dinosaur. For all practical purposes, I was extinct.

Twenty years ago, it didn't seem a kid was as quick to pull a gun. I know they weren't as quick to pull a trigger. Not just the job, but the time had passed me by.

"That bad?" Deanna asked. She was in her street clothes. Tiny. Petite. Unbearably beautiful.

"Yep."

"You want to talk about it?"

"Nope."

"You want a hug?"

I opened my arms. "Yep."

She snuggled in against my chest and stayed there. Her head tucked up under my chin where I could smell her hair. Her arms snugly around me. Not moving.

We stayed there for a long time, leaned against the closed and empty beer bar in the relatively vacant section of the club. It was almost five. I didn't care. I wasn't moving. I would write the incident reports tomorrow. Post date them. Or maybe I wouldn't. Maybe I would just hold on to Deanna until my shift was over. Maybe I would hold her a little longer. It was well after five before I felt like saying anything at all. The night shift was gone. The customers who were leaving in droves let in a grimy piercing light through the doors.

"Let me walk you out," I said.

We walked to her car, side by side. I carried her bag. She kept her arm through mine, carrying me.

There was a news van setting up for a shot in the

parking lot. Another story about cabdriver extortion, or a new law in effect, or how much money we all made, or what sort of lousy, degenerate people we all were.

I put Deanna's bag in the trunk of her car and pressed it closed. I stood there, leaning on the trunk with both hands.

"How's that new TV?" I asked.

Deanna kissed me on the shoulder, then rested her forehead there.

She handed me the keys and got in the passenger side. I got in behind the wheel and adjusted the seat and started the car. She leaned her head on my shoulder and intertwined her fingers in mine on the gear shift.

A huge van with FBI stenciled on the side followed a pair of black government sedans into the parking lot. Several more government sedans followed. A few sped around back and to the side doors. Metro Police cars, lights flashing, blocked off the parking lot and the street in front of Brass Poles.

The van doors opened and a swarm of FBI agents in their FBI windbreakers and tactical gear, piled out. FBI agents were leaping from the sedans, their compact black HK sub-machine guns held at the ready.

Deanna and I watched.

I turned off the engine and opened the door.

Deanna held me by the arm and shook her head.

"I've got to go," I said. I got out of the car.

I walked in through the front doors past an FBI agent who held his weapon at the ready, preventing anyone from leaving. Apparently they hadn't thought to secure the building against anyone coming in. The agent shouted,

"Hey!" at me. I kept going. I got inside just in time to see a stout agent crush the office door with a ram, and the door cave inward. FBI agents were scurrying around in an agitated state, herding entertainers into the dressing room. Shouting commands at the few customers who remained. Waving their guns around like bandits in a fifties Western.

Some of the entertainers were being drug, an FBI agent on each arm, squirming and screaming profanity, to the dressing room. That's where I headed.

The dressing room was like an ant hill that had been kicked by a sadistic child, only louder.

Male and female FBI agents were holding terrified girls, in varying states of undress, at gunpoint in one corner, while other agents used pry bars to tear open lockers and spill their contents onto the floor.

Several of the girls were crying. Several were cursing. Several were standing, dejected, resigned. Someone screamed my name.

A girl, in only a g-string, was face down on the floor while four FBI agents attempted to put her in handcuffs. One agent probably could have done it easy. Four were getting in each other's way. The girl had her hands tucked up under her chest. One Agent was kneeling on her neck, pinning her to the ground. She couldn't have gotten her hands out from under her if she wanted. The four agents were still holding their sub-machine guns, which wasn't making it any easier.

Several other girls were trying to come to her aid and being shoved violently back by more FBI agents.

I grabbed one FBI agent who was kneeling on the girl's neck, by the back of his collar, and slung him into a bank of lockers.

The remaining Agents got off the girl and pointed their guns at me, screaming; "Down! Down! Down! Get down! Let me see your hands!"

I showed them my hands. I put them out to my sides, palms out. It was the second time in the same day guns were pointing at me. I liked it even less this time.

The girl who had been on the ground scrambled to the cover of her friends.

The agent who I had slung into the lockers was on his feet now. He was behind me. I heard his retractable baton extend with a snap. The long, metal, flexible kind. This was going to hurt.

The first strike hit me in the back of my leg, just above the knee. I didn't go down. He should have hit me lower, on the joint, busted some of the tendons. Fucking rookie.

I stood there with my arms out, making like Christ on the cross, as long as I could. Some of the other FBI Agents had joined in. Another emptied half a can of pepper spray into my face. I don't remember much after that. Someone hit me high on the neck with their baton. Everything went dim. I think they tazed me.

I remembered when they stopped hitting me and applied the handcuffs. I remembered some of the girls crying and screaming my name and threatening to sue everyone from the FBI to the president.

I remembered telling the girls that I was okay. But in truth, I don't remember if I had actually told them, or I had only thought about it. I was pretty messed up.

A couple of paramedics attended to me the best they

could. Their bedside manner was horrible. One kept looking at the other and shaking his head like I wasn't going to
make it. I would make it, I knew, but I probably would
wish I hadn't by the next day. Everything was sort of numb
now. It wouldn't be in a few hours. The adrenaline would
wear off and then it was going to hurt, a lot. Fuck it.
Nothing I could do about it now.

I thought about how worried Susan would be when
I didn't call her that night. I wouldn't even be able to call
her collect from jail, I knew. I didn't have her mother's
number with me. Jail phones didn't allow long distance
information.

I knew Kiko would be all right for a few days until
someone figured out what happened to me and went to
take care of her. Robert, I thought. Robert would hop my
back gate and go in through the back door and make sure
she had food and water. I could count on Robert. She had
enough to last her a couple days. She would be worried
too, I knew.

I wished the girls would stop crying. I was okay. I
wished someone would tell them I was okay.

After a while, they rode me to the hospital in the
ambulance. The emergency room doctor made them take
my hand cuffs off so they could set my broken fingers. He
set my jaw, but didn't have to wire it, and had some temporary stuff put on my teeth to keep the roots from being
exposed. He sewed up the cuts on the back of my head and
under my eye and on the inside of my lips. He packed and
reset my nose. I slept through most of it.

They put me in the infirmary when I got to the jail.
Kind of them, I thought. Let me heal up a few days before

dropping me into the general population.

Assault on a Federal officer. I knew I would be in for a while.

I was wrong.

A guard came in calling my name.

The guard had asked me if I could walk. I was a little curious about that, myself. I could walk. I could barely see, both my eyes were swollen to slits, but I could walk.

They had given me something for pain in the hospital, and by the time it wore off, I was wishing the FBI had shot me instead.

It took about two hours to out-process me, and when they let me out the little side door to the jail, Deanna was waiting.

The look on her face, stung a little. There was a heavy amount of repulsion in the look. She started crying.

I hobbled over to her and said, "I'm okay," Between my aching jaw, my swollen lips, and my broken teeth, even I could barely understand what I had said.

Deanna started laughing.

"Come on," she said and led me to her car which was parked illegally on the curb across the street. She walked slowly, holding my arm, as I hobbled, very conscious of each and every step.

A big, beautiful, new Mercedes being driven by a man who looked like he should be driving a big, beautiful, new Mercedes, was protectively double parked just outside of Deanna's car. She gave the driver a wave. He waved back and pulled away.

Deanna helped me into her car. It took me a couple of trys to find how I could bend, and how I couldn't. She put the seat belt on me and got behind the wheel.

"How did you get me out?" I asked. When I spoke really slowly you could almost understand me.

"Jerry, Deanna said as she pulled into traffic.

"Jerry?"

"He's one of my customers. The guy in the Mercedes."

"Good customer," I said.

Deanna sniffled and laughed and kept her eyes on the road.

"What time is it?" I asked.

"Almost seven," Deanna said.

"What day?"

She laughed again. It was a nervous sound. Not at all happy. "You've been in about thirteen hours."

"Very good customer," I said.

"He's a Federal judge. He says he's going to have your case assigned to his court. He says he's going to destroy the Agents who did this to you."

"Good, then we'll be even."

She didn't laugh this time.

"I've got to call Susan."

"I think I should take you to the hospital."

"I've been. Just get me home."


I got through my phone conversation with Susan using grunts and humms. Fortunately, that's how most my conversations were, and after the first few times she asked me what was the matter, and I wouldn't tell her, she gave up and talked for almost an hour about the preparations for her mother, and how her sister was holding up. She didn't sound so good. I should have been there.

Deanna stayed the night. It was not at all how I had always envisioned it. I couldn't sleep. She told me she could get me some Loritab. I told her no.

After about twelve hours of sweating in pain, and her staying up, beside me the whole time, wiping my head with a damp cloth and looking down on me with those big, sad eyes, I said okay, give me the drug.

I took a Loritab and the world got good and soft, and I slept.

When I woke up, Deanna was there, sleeping on the bed beside me. Nope, not at all the way I had imagined it.

I slept again, then woke and Deanna offered me another Loritab. I said no. Hell no. I could get used to that stuff in a hurry. I had too many friends heading down that road.

When I woke the next time, I was surprised at how good I felt. Good isn't the word, but I didn't feel appreciably worse than the time I had gone five rounds with Chuck Liddell. I probably wasn't much uglier, either.

I sent Deanna home. I couldn't have her in the house when I got feeling even a little better. She argued, but she did what I said. She always had.

The light was blinking on the answering machine. I had ignored it for two days. Now I pressed play.

It was a message from someone I had never heard of before. He said he was the new general manager of Brass Poles. He said my services were no longer required, effectively immediately. I erased the message.

I got my teeth fixed permanently and kept ice on

my face and had my stitches removed, and three weeks later Susan was home with me. She had wrapped up her mother's affairs in San Diego, and had come home. It had been too long.

We sat on the couch and watched TV. At eight o;clock, she asked me if I was going to get ready for work.

I said, "No."

She looked at me for a long moment. She didn't smile. "That's good," she said.

*Destiny is a name often given in retrospect to choices*
*that had dramatic consequences.*
*- J. K. Rowling*

# THE END

*I*t all may be over now, and not just for me. The FBI raid that temporarily shut the doors of Cheetahs in May 2003, may well be the beginning of the end for the famous strip club. Mike Galardi's penchant for hiring managers by the perks they could provide finally came back to haunt him in a profoundly ironic way.

"Big Tony Montagna," Cheetahs head of security, was hired on the basis that he was able to give Mike information about an upcoming vice raid in San Diego. (His claim: he had access to a dirty cop.) Based on this information, Tony was made head of security of both Cheetahs in San Diego and Las Vegas. Tony had never worked in the nightclub or security business before. He was not overly bright, but he was smart enough to fool Galardi.

So, who was Tony? As it turns out, Tony was an FBI informant—a rat—and Mike Galardi had welcomed him with open arms, and an all-access pass to the Cheetahs infrastructure.

During the Operation G-sting raid, the Feds took everything. Every scrap of paper from Galardi's offices in Las Vegas and San Diego.

The basis for the raid? Political corruption and buying of political power. Politicians in both cities are also targets of the FBI investigation.

According to the FBI, Mike Galardi had been paying numerous city council members, in both cities, for favorable decisions on zoning and such.

Gee, no kidding.

It took the FBI two years, an undercover snitch, and a shit-load of money to figure that one out? All they had to do was ask.

Anyone who had been employed by Cheetahs for more than a month, no doubt had been subjected to politicians and their boasts of how they "take care" of Mike or "own this place" or how the new club wouldn't even exist without them. Hell, for the promise of immunity and a cup of Starbucks, half the Cheetahs employees would have gleefully sold everyone involved—on both sides—down the river years ago. And who could blame them? Most of the politicians I have had experience with are slimy, inconsiderate, rude, greedy, good-for-nothing leeches who deserve no better. (Everyone's got an opinion.)

My former employer, on the other hand, was a different matter. I was employed by Mike Galardi for more than twelve years, and I am a Samurai in my soul (if not by birth).

A Samurai defends his retainer to the death, and I had often—weekly—put my life on the line for Galardi and his club over the years. I was in his employ, taking his money. It was my duty to throw myself under the bus for him whenever necessary; there had been many buses. (The buses continue coming. I am, of this writing, named in a lawsuit against Cheetahs and employees for a beating delivered to a pair of suspects. My total involvement in that particular incident consisted of getting hit in the head by one of the suspects while trying to save their lives. However, I was there that night. I am not absolved regardless of my attempts or intent.)

In June 2003, I was dismissed from Cheetahs, released from service by Mr. White, the latest in a long succession of general managers. With my dismissal also goes my loyalty. I am no longer honor bound to protect Mike Galardi or Cheetahs. I feel that if there is any justice in the world (a notion in which I am not a firm believer), Mike Galardi will be singing happy birthday to his children through wire-reinforced glass for many years to come.

I don't think Mike is going to fare well in prison; he is used to getting his way in all matters—an arrogant braggart of a man who grew up choking on his father's silver spoon, surrounded by a host of sycophantic parasites who were paid well to laugh at his jokes and coo at every pearl of wisdom dribbled from his lips.

As the story of "Operation G-sting" (as the FBI and press has titled the Cheetahs investigation) unfolds, I think what strikes me most, is how little the politicians went for. The numbers being mentioned are in the five, to ten thousand dollar range, for favors rendered. Five thousand dollars? How do you sell out your city for five thousand dollars? Five thousand dollars isn't even a single insurance payment on his Lamborghini, for a guy like Mike Galardi. Five thousand dollars? I mean, really, what are you going to do with five thousand dollars? Politicians sold out their city for the equivalent of a big-screen television. Small minds, small ambition.

Speaking of small minds and ambition, the extensive Cheetahs management crew may be looking at some very hard times. Though certainly not innocent of the crimes of pimping, pandering, drug dealing, and a host of other offenses, their general lack of ambition in the FBI-investigated crimes, at least will probably spare them some well-deserved prison time. However, the Cheetahs management future career choices are, in a massive understatement, severely limited. After years of making a quarter-million dollars per year for following Mike Galardi around like the entourage of a certain good-hearted heavyweight fighter who doesn't know any better, what exactly are they going to put on their resume?

It appears now that Mike Galardi's clubs are being taken over by his father, Jack Galardi, a man who though dogged by rumors of ties to organized crime (why the FBI began Operation G-sting in the first place?) remains a non-felon. Jack Galardi seems to have another advantage over his son Mike. He is not cheap. The city of Las Vegas determined that Jack Galardi was welcome to take over Mike's club's after paying a fine of just more than one million dollars. One million dollars to Galardi is akin to someone who makes fifty thousand dollars per year getting caught parked in a handicapped parking space, or what I would call the bargain of the century.

My twenty-year career has blessed and cursed me at the same time. I have been exposed to the best and worst humanity has to offer. I have been befriended by men and women who would give their lives, and all that entails, without question, or even my bidding. I have met the others also.

I have witnessed, and been party to, acts that will exclude me from a place in heaven, but I have never betrayed the trust of those who have trusted me. If nothing else, I have earned that claim. That is as much as I could have ever hoped for.

*Just because your voice reaches halfway around the world*
*doesn't mean you are wiser than when it reached*
*only to the end of the bar.*
*- Edward R. Murrow*

## LESSONS LEARNED

*N*ow it is clear to me that my twenty years as a strip club bouncer gave me much more than money and sex and violence and cheap thrills. It afforded me the opportunity to live my life in pursuit of my goals and dreams: Not something I see many people in other lines of work having the opportunity to do.

Being a strip club bouncer afforded me the opportunity to open my own bar (The Lighter Side Cafe at San Diego State College), to learn, and practice, the Japanese language, to learn to write HTML and Java Script (before WYSIWYG editors) and post my own web sites from which I advertised and sold the screenplays I learned to write, the video tapes I learned to shoot and edit, and the CD ROM enhanced text books I learned to publish. I learned how to invest money in both the stock markets and in real estate, which taught me how to manage rental properties and be a benevolent and efficient slumlord.

Besides the money that allowed me to invest in all

these ventures, the time the job afforded me was invaluable. A dozen, two minute incidents (fights, customer attitude adjustments, collections, etc...) in an eight hour shift leaves a lot of standing around time. Being a strip club bouncer isn't, as they say, brain surgery. You spend most of your time watching and listening and anticipating problems before they happen.

For years, when I was working the afternoon shift at Cheetahs, you would never see me without a book of some sort (how I learned to operate a computer), or my language flash cards (how I learned Japanese), or hefting a $CO_2$ canister (how I put an inch on my upper arms one year—curls for the girls).

My work library read like the "how-to" section at Barnes & Noble; "How To Write HTML," "How To Write Java Script," "How to Write a Screenplay," "The Macintosh Bible," "Adobe Photoshop Bible," "Quark Express [Bible]," "ClarisWorks Bible," "The Idiot's Guide to Macromedia Flash," "The Idiot's Guide to Getting Published," "[The Idiot's Guide to] Learning Japanese,"... Like I said, I had a lot of time on my hands, and I couldn't see wasting it. I have always maintained that if you could read, and comprehend what you read, there is nothing you can not learn.

Later, when I began working night shifts and there was no more time for reading, or flash cards, or curling $CO_2$ canisters, my education continued. I learned how to sum up a man at a glance—see into his soul before even he knew what was there. I learned how to determine if a man was going to need a hard sell, a soft sell, a friend, or an authority figure, to prompt him into doing the right thing.

I can instantly see if a man has violence, or fear, or anger, or pain in his heart. I can tell if a man has been caught up in circumstances beyond his control, or has entered into the circumstances with malice in mind. All this—this education, this knowledge—has allowed me to smile genuinely and proudly when an offended customer shouts back at me, after being ejected from the bar, that I will never be anything more than a bouncer. I can smile because, if that were truly the end sum of my life, I know I could have done much worse.

Far more important than what I have learned from customers, is what I have learned from the entertainers; I have learned what true tenacity and toughness are. I have had a priceless glimpse into the minds and hearts of women. From the millions upon millions of complaints I have fielded, I have learned exactly when, and how, and why women lose interest in a man. I know what women find most attractive, and what they find most repulsive. Unfortunately, like most of us, I am much better at gaining knowledge than applying it, and much better at giving advice than taking it.

In a strip club, you spend an incredible amount of time speaking with your co-workers about what you will do when you get out of the business. Discussing dreams, goals, working out business plans, and bouncing ideas off one another. It seems everyone in the business has that in common: goals beyond the strip club. I can't fathom what it would be like not to have a lofty, "impossible" goal to strive for—a dream—and like-minded individuals to share that dream with.

I have met the best people in my life as a strip club

bouncer. People who provided me with insight to worlds I would have never known otherwise. I have met men and women who have sacrificed themselves for me, and I am in awe of every one of them.

There were the others too, obviously. The lower forms of life which people traditionally associate with strip clubs, but truly, those memories pale in comparison to the amazing deeds and acts I have seen.

By far, the most valuable and important thing I have learned over the past twenty years is the most valuable and important thing anyone can learn: their destiny.

I learned it is my destiny to tell stories.

For twenty years I was a strip club bouncer, and now I am a story teller. The funny thing is, that destiny that took me all these years to realize, has been staring me in the face for the vast majority of my life. It seems so simple now (in retrospect), what I was born to do.

The largest influence in my life has always been the movies. My fantasies, as a youth, always revolved around the larger-than-life heroes who said what they felt, and did what they said. John Wayne, Anthony Quinn, Lee Marvin, Humphrey Bogart, Robert Mitchum, Clint Eastwood...these were men (who played the men) who never backed down, never quit. This is where I learned to stand up proud, and tall, and never hold back. Rocky Balboa, Travis Bickle, Ripley, Conan...taught me to never quit—never—no matter how dire or hopeless or impossible the situation. They all taught me how to be "cool"—how to walk, and talk, and sneer and shoot back snappy one-liners in response to insults. They taught me how to say what I meant, and then follow through with what I said—damn the consequences.

So that is how I will spend the rest of my life; I will tell stories in the form of screenplays, and novels, and books, and make films that make people proud, and happy, and make them think, and laugh, and cry, and joyful, and learn, and remember.... That is what twenty years as a strip club bouncer has done for me.

I have been criticized for my life being one long fantasy. I have been told that there is no basis in reality for being a warrior and a strip club bouncer and a story teller...and I agree. But then, that's something else I've learned: Reality is for those with no imagination.

*"In the end,
we will remember not the words of our enemies,
but the silence of our friends."
- Martin Luther King Jr.*

## AUTHOR END NOTE:

*I*t has been two years since I was fired from Cheetahs Las Vegas. In retrospect, I can see now that it was clearly time for me to move on.

Eight different strip clubs—over 20 years—and I never quit a single one. It's been a hell of a ride.

The thing about a job like being a bouncer in a strip club is, no one in their right mind could ever justify leaving the position voluntarily. There is a good possibility that never again in my life will I be able to make that much money, for such little work, doing something I enjoyed so much. How could I walk away from a job where I was paid obscene amounts of cash for watching strikingly beautiful young women take their clothes off for eight hours at a time, and every once in a while, get to slap the living piss out of someone who desperately needed it? In my case, I couldn't walk away. I had always maintained that they would have to drag me away from that job by my heels, kicking and screaming all the way. In the end, they didn't exactly have to drag me, but they did have to ask me to leave. I don't know if I could have ever done it on my own.

Does it sound like I miss it? I do. I miss being a friend and confidant, and protector...to the exceptional sorts I met over the years. I don't think I would have had the opportunity to met such a diversity of individuals in any other line of work.

That's one thing about the strip club business, it's definitely full of characters.

Jim
Big John
Loni
Jay
Tommy
Blake
Clarence

You are missed.

Save my place. I'll be along directly.

## ACKNOWLEDGEMENTS:

*I* am, without a doubt, the most fortunate man alive. How do I define fortune? What is my criteria? I judge my fortune by those who call me friend, and those who don't.

*Robert*: the most energetic, optimistic, hardworking individual on earth. Robert inspires me to do more.

*Deanna*: a reoccurring character in everything I write (screenplays, novels, short stories...). She is the model for femininity burned indelibly in my mind.

*Jessica*: the most determined individual I have ever met. Jessica not only gave me the inspiration for my finest screenplay, but inspired my life's mantra as well.

*Kelly*: The closest to altruistic my belief system will allow.

*Susan,* my wife: wholly dedicated.

A person would be blessed to know any one of these people. That makes me many times blessed, and the most fortunate man alive.

To all those who showed me hate, you gave me a cause to fight against.

To all those who showed me love, you have my love in return.

To Mike Galardi:
Without your defining characteristics
—greed and ignorance—
this book would never have been possible.

We hope you enjoyed Stripped.
Spread the word. Tell a friend.

Contact the author at
satsupress@cox.net

www.strippedbook.com

About the Author:

Brent Kenton Jordan worked as a strip club bouncer in eight different clubs, 40 hours per week, for twenty years.

*"I've seen the devil of violence, and the devil of greed, and the devil of hot desire; but, by all the stars! These were strong, lusty, red-eyed devils, that swayed and drove men - men, I tell you."*

*- Conrad, Heart of Darkness*